2015

Preliminary Overview of the Economies
of Latin America and the Caribbean

UNITED NATIONS

Alicia Bárcena
Executive Secretary

Antonio Prado
Deputy Executive Secretary

Daniel Titelman
Chief, Economic Development Division

Ricardo Pérez
Chief, Publications and Web Services Division

The *Preliminary Overview of the Economies of Latin America and the Caribbean* is an annual publication prepared by the Economic Development Division of the Economic Commission for Latin America and the Caribbean (ECLAC). This 2015 edition was prepared under the supervision of Daniel Titelman, Chief of the Division, while Jurgen Weller, Senior Economic Affairs Officer, was responsible for its overall coordination.

In the preparation of this edition, the Economic Development Division was assisted by the Statistics Division, the ECLAC subregional headquarters in Mexico City and Port of Spain, and the Commission's country offices in Bogota, Brasilia, Buenos Aires, Montevideo and Washington, D.C.

This briefing paper was prepared by Daniel Titelman with inputs provided by the following exerts: Cecilia Vera (global economic trends and external sector), Claudia de Camino (external sector), Ricardo Martner, Michael Hanni and Ivonne González (fiscal policy), Ramón Pineda (economic activity, prices, and monetary, exchange-rate and macroprudential policies), Rodrigo Cárcamo and Alejandra Acevedo (monetary, exchange-rate and macroprudential policies), Claudio Aravena (economic activity), Alda Díaz (prices) and Jürgen Weller (employment and wages). The economic projections were produced by Ramón Pineda, Claudio Aravena, Pablo Carvallo, Alejandra Acevedo, Yusuke Tateno and Matías Rojas with input from the ECLAC subregional headquarters and national offices. Alejandra Acevedo, Alda Díaz and María Zambrano were responsible for the processing and presentation of the statistical data and graphical presentations.

The country notes are based on studies conducted by the following experts: Olga Lucía Acosta, Juan Carlos Ramírez and Luis Javier Uribe (Colombia), Dillon Alleyne (Jamaica), Anahí Amar and Daniel Vega (Argentina), Rodrigo Cárcamo (Peru), Cameron Daneshvar (Dominican Republic and Honduras), Stefanie Garry (El Salvador and Guatemala), Randolph Gilbert (Haiti), Sonia Gontero (Paraguay), Michael Hanni (Plurinational State of Bolivia), Michael Hendrickson (Bahamas and Belize), Cornelia Kaldewei (Ecuador), Álvaro Lalanne and Florencia Pietrafesa (Uruguay), Ricardo Martner (Chile), Sheldon McLean (Eastern Caribbean Currency Union and Guyana), Rodolfo Minzer (Panama), Carlos Mussi (Brazil), Ramón Padilla (Costa Rica), Machel Pantin (Suriname and Trinidad and Tobago), Juan Carlos Rivas (Mexico), Indira Romero (Cuba), Jesús Santamaría (El Salvador), Nyasha Skerrette (Barbados) and Francisco Villarreal (Nicaragua). Michael Hanni and José Luis Germán reviewed the Caribbean country notes. Georgina Cipoletta, Juan Pablo Jiménez and Esteban Pérez participated in the review of the country notes for Latin America.

The country notes are available online at www.eclac.org.

The cut-off date for the information presented in this publication was 30 November 2015.

Explanatory notes:

- Three dots (...) indicate that data are not available or are not separately reported.
- A dash (-) indicates that the amount is nil or negligible.
- A full stop (.) is used to indicate decimals.
- The word "dollars" refers to United States dollars, unless otherwise specified.
- A slash (/) between years (e.g. 2013/2014) indicates a 12-month period falling between the two years.
- Individual figures and percentages in tables may not always add up to the corresponding total because of rounding.

United Nations publication
ISBN: 978-92-1-121911-1 (print)
ISBN: 978-92-1-057525-6 (pdf)
ISBN: 978-92-1-358023-3 (ePub)
LC/G.2655-P
Sales No.: E.16.II.G.2
Copyright © United Nations, 2015
All rights reserved.
Printed at United Nations, Santiago, Chile
S.15-01386

Contents

Executive summary

A. Global economic trends

Global economic growth is still sluggish, and will remain so in the medium term. The world economy grew by 2.4% in 2015, slightly less than the 2.6% posted in 2014. In 2016 the global economy is expected to recover somewhat, with expansion of 2.9%.

The 2015 growth performance was marked by a slowdown in the emerging economies, whose growth declined from 4.3% in 2014 to 3.8% in 2015, and particularly China, which grew by less than 7% for the first time since 1990 (around 6.8%). This contrasts with India's growth trajectory, which has been rising steadily since 2013 and reached 7.2% in 2015. The growth rate for the group of developed countries, meanwhile, though still well below those of the developing world, edged up from 1.7% in 2014 to 1.9% in 2015. In 2016 the emerging economies are expected to return to 2014 growth rates, at 4.3%. Growth in the developed countries will tick up to 2.2%.

Global growth projections for 2016 are highly subject to the trajectory of the Chinese economy, which has been slowing heavily. Amid mounting uncertainty arising from financial volatility in China, combined with its shift from an investment-based to a consumption-based growth strategy, projections point to a deceleration to around 6.4%. A sharper slowdown in China in 2016 would bring down global growth projections, as well.

World trade has been growing even more slowly than the global economy, with an expansion of just 1.5% in volume during the first nine months of 2015 relative to the year-earlier period, this being the lowest rate since the international financial crisis of 2008 and 2009. Global trade volumes are expected to climb modestly in 2016, by around 2.5%.

Prices for raw materials, a key factor for the economies of the region, continued to decline in 2015, with no significant change expected for 2016. Between January 2011 and October 2015, prices for metals and energy (oil, gas and coal) fell by almost 50%, and food prices by 30%. Energy products saw the largest decline in 2015, with prices dropping by 24% between January and October, during which period prices for metals fell by 21% and for agricultural commodities by 10%.

The behaviour of raw materials prices reflects supply and demand shifts (heavily influenced by growth performance in China), as well as the effects of volatility and financial speculation in these goods as they have become increasingly used as financial assets.

Financial market volatility increased in 2015, in the first half of the year because of problems in Greece and in the second half because of developments in China. This greater volatility, combined with an interest rate hike in the United States, augurs tighter global liquidity and a gradual rise in the cost of financial resources on the international markets.

In 2015 the emerging economies felt the effects of decreasing availability of financial flows given the uncertainty and volatility that prevailed to a greater or lesser extent for most of the year. Cumulative total flows to emerging economies for the year up to October 2015 were 65% less than the amount registered in the prior-year period.

Financial flows to emerging markets are unlikely to pick up in 2016, owing to tighter global liquidity conditions in the wake of monetary policy normalization in the United States and a degree of risk aversion arising from uncertainty prevailing on several fronts.

B. The external sector

The prices of the region's commodity exports continued to weaken in the second half of 2015, hurting the terms of trade. For the region as a whole, the terms of trade are estimated to have deteriorated by 9% over the year. For the Central American and Caribbean countries (excluding Trinidad and Tobago), the terms of trade improved by 5% and 2%, respectively. By contrast, those of the South American countries fell by 13%. The worst hit countries were the exporters of hydrocarbons (down by 27%). The terms of trade for Latin America as a whole look set to decline further in 2016, although not nearly as heavily as in 2015.

Despite the worsening trade balance, the balance-of-payments current account deficit narrowed in nominal terms, from US$ 175 billion to US$ 169 billion. This improvement was offset by the reduction in regional GDP measured in dollars, however, so the current account deficit as a percentage of GDP widened in 2015 to 3.5%.

Among the current account components, the merchandise trade balance deficit widened very significantly from US$ 4 billion in 2014 to US$ 38.2 billion in 2015. This is the first time since 2001 that the trade balance has been in deficit for two years running. The wider gap reflected a sharp 14% fall in the value of the region's exports and a 10% decline in import values, whose absolute magnitude was insufficient to offset the drop in exports in 2015. That drop in export value is explained basically by the 15% fall in Latin American export prices. The decrease in import value reflected a 7% drop in prices, owing mainly to energy products, and a 3% contraction in volumes, given the moderate level of activity in several of the region's economies.

The net inflow of financial resources to the region totalled 2.8% of GDP in 2015, which was insufficient to fully finance the current account deficit. As a result, the region as a whole used international reserves amounting to 0.7% of GDP to cover the shortfall.

Foreign direct investment (FDI) fell by around 22% in 2015 from its 2014 level and is expected to stand at around US$ 107 billion at the end of the year. Net regional inflows of portfolio capital —basically investments in bonds and shares— also retreated sharply from the year-earlier levels. In 2014, these flows had attained just over US$ 115 billion, and a 40% fall is expected for 2015, bringing them to around US$ 70 billion by year-end.

Latin America and Caribbean debt issues on international markets fell substantially in 2015, especially in the second half of the year. Third-quarter issues totalled just US$ 10 billion, 63% down on the year-earlier period, and the lowest quarterly level since June 2009 when the global financial crisis was at its height. Considering cumulative issues over 12 months at the sector level, the year-on-year declines at November amount to 75% for banks, 48% for the private sector, 46% for quasi-sovereigns, 13% for sovereigns, and 7% for supranationals.

The region's average sovereign risk rose slightly in 2015. As measured by the Emerging Market Bond Index Global (EMBIG), the region's average sovereign risk spread rose by 53 basis points between January and November 2014, to 561 basis points.

C. Economic activity

The Latin American and Caribbean region's GDP contracted by 0.4% in 2015, which translated into a 1.5% downturn in per capita GDP and represented the poorest performance since 2009. As in 2014, large differences were seen in economic activity levels between subregions and between countries. The shrinking economic activity at the regional level reflected the downturn in the South American economies, which, as a group, went from growth of 0.6% in 2014 to contraction of 1.6% in 2015. The subregion's performance was heavily influenced by the negative growth posted by Brazil and the Bolivarian Republic of Venezuela.

The Central American economies continued to expand in 2015, with a rate of 4.4% expected for the year overall. The inclusion of Mexico in this group of countries brings the average growth rate to 2.9%. The English- and Dutch-speaking Caribbean economies experienced an uptick in growth, from 0.7% in 2014 to 1.0% in 2015.

Consistently with the pattern in recent years, domestic demand slowed heavily, with a drop in investment and consumption. In regional terms, domestic demand was down by 0.7% in 2015, with a contraction in private consumption (-0.3%) and gross fixed capital formation (-4.2%) and a meagre gain in public consumption (0.7%).

Like economic activity overall, the various components of aggregate demand were sharply differentiated by subregion in 2015. With respect to 2014 figures, private consumption shrank 1.6% in South America, but rose 4.6% in Central America. Similarly, public consumption almost flatlined in South America, at 0.1%, but climbed 4.4% in Central America. Gross fixed capital formation fell heavily in South America (7.2%), but climbed 7% in Central America.

A five-quarter run of contraction in gross fixed capital formation beginning in the second quarter of 2014 has brought this variable's GDP share down by 1.5 percentage points, from 21.5% in 2013 to 20.0% in 2015.

Weak domestic demand has been reflected in a 1.1% fall in goods and services imports in real terms, as a result of lower consumption and slack investment in the region overall. Meanwhile, goods and services exports climbed 2.5% in real terms. Given that the region's real imports slowed faster than in 2014, net exports made a slightly larger contribution to growth than last year.

The regional slowdown also shows a markedly sectoral bias. Although all the sectors have slowed, construction, manufacturing and electricity generation, gas and water, as a group, contracted by 1.8% in 2015 on top of a 0.3% decline in 2014, while the primary and tertiary sectors expanded 1.7% and 0.5%, respectively. As a result, the contribution of the secondary sector to value added growth was negative by 0.43 percentage points, of which the manufacturing sector alone accounted for 0.34 percentage points. The tertiary sector is still the largest contributor, bringing 0.38 percentage points to value added growth, while the contribution of the primary sector held steady at 0.12 percentage points in 2015.

By subregion, in Central America, construction, manufacturing and electricity generation, gas and water, as a group, expanded 0.6%, but it shrank by 0.3% in South America. Manufacturing performance was worst in South America, where it contracted by 4.2% with respect to 2014, reflecting almost zero or negative growth rates in Argentina, the Bolivarian Republic of Venezuela, Brazil, Chile, Colombia, Ecuador and Peru.

D. Employment

The economic slowdown has had a heavier impact on employment dynamics in 2015 than in 2014. In 2015, the decline in labour participation stopped, and the larger number of individuals seeking income in the job market amid slack labour demand pushed up both open unemployment and time-related underemployment. A growing proportion of employment appeared in low-productivity activities, particularly own-account work, and creation of wage employment was sparse. As a result, average labour productivity declined sharply.

Like growth, labour market performance varied between the region's countries in 2015. Although the unemployment rate rose in the regional weighted average, employment and unemployment rates are not yet worsening in most countries. Nonetheless, labour market conditions increasingly deteriorated over the course of the year.

In this context, the unemployment rate is expected to increase to 6.6% in 2015, representing an estimated 1.5 million additional urban unemployed and pushing the total up to 14.7 million. Wage employment rose by 0.4%, far less than the 0.8% posted in 2014. Growth in own-account work was 2.8% in the first half of 2015, which translates into a downturn in average employment quality.

Real wages showed a slight rise of 1.2% in the average for the region overall in 2015. This was a smaller gain than in 2014, although the pattern is very uneven between countries. The heterogeneous performance of real wages chiefly reflects the different trajectories of inflation in the countries over the year.

E. Policies

1. Fiscal policy

Increasing fiscal strains in 2015 —for the first time since 2009, all the countries of Latin America are running fiscal deficits— have led most of the countries in the region to begin entrenching their public finances. At the central government level, the average fiscal outcome in 2015 is expected to be a primary deficit of 1% of GDP and an overall deficit (including public debt interest payments) of 3% of GDP.

The heterogeneity of the macroeconomic performance and production specialization of the region's countries is reflected in an array of fiscal outcomes. In commodity-exporting countries, a substantial drop in fiscal revenues resulting from lower export commodity prices was offset by higher tax revenues and proportional adjustments in public spending.

In Central America and the Caribbean, public finances have benefited from a significant and positive twofold fiscal shock, with fairly vigorous growth and lower oil outlays.

Despite the heavier pressure from the public deficits, Latin America's public debt increased only slightly to an average of 34.3% of GDP in 2015, still a comparatively low level. However, the rising trend has much sharper in Brazil, where public debt increased by 7 percentage points over the year, this being attributable to a worsening fiscal deficit and high rates of interest being paid on public securities interest rates. Debt in the Caribbean countries has generally trended upward over the past half-decade and now averages about 80% of GDP, with Jamaica having the largest public debt at 131% of GDP.

Reflecting fiscal consolidation, public spending has fallen in relation to GDP, especially capital spending, which dropped by an average of 0.4 points of GDP, in contrast to the substantial increases of 2014. At the same time, although the averages were not much affected, there was a substantial increase in public debt service in several countries. In Brazil, almost the entirety of the rise in public spending in 2015 was accounted for by growth in interest payments (2.7 points of GDP). In other countries (Costa Rica and the Dominican Republic), this expenditure represented a share of over 15%.

Current primary spending growth moderated on average, after rising continuously as a share of GDP for a number of years. There was a sharp fall in hydrocarbon-exporting countries (1.1 GDP points), contrasting with substantial rises in food-exporting countries. In the Caribbean, average current primary spending was up by a substantial 0.6 GDP points, with the largest rises in Bahamas, Barbados, Guyana and Trinidad and Tobago.

Fiscal revenues deteriorated slightly in 2015, mainly because of a drop in income from non-renewable natural resources. The collapse of the international crude oil price dealt a blow to the public accounts of the region's producing countries. However, this decline was partly offset in a number of countries by increased tax revenues. On average, Latin America succeeded in increasing tax pressure by 0.2 percentage points of GDP in 2015.

In the Central American countries, tax revenues held relatively steady, and in the Caribbean they rose slightly.

2. Prices and exchange-rate and monetary policies

Inflation was much the same in 2015 as in 2014 in the region overall, with patterns diverging sharply between the north and south of the region and between the first and second halves of the year. In the first 10 months of the year, inflation in Latin America and the Caribbean was slightly higher in the year-earlier period, with a cumulative price rise of 6.6% as compared to 6.5% the year before and 6.3% at year-end 2014. The regional inflation rate was lower in the first five months of the year, at 6.0%, than in late 2014, but the situation was reversed in the second half as price rises accelerated, showing the effects of heavy currency depreciations in some of the region's countries.

In the cases of Central America, Mexico and the English- and Dutch-speaking Caribbean, the trend of slowing inflation since 2013 became more pronounced in 2015, so that the cumulative change in the consumer price index for the subregion comprising the economies of Central America and Mexico in the 12 months to October dropped from 4.3% in 2014 to 2.7% in 2015. In the South American economies, conversely, inflation has continued to gather pace, so that the cumulative figure for the 12 months to October rose from 7.6% in 2014 to 8.5% in 2015.

Changes in international conditions, including falling prices for primary goods and mounting volatility in international financial markets, together with trends in domestic prices, have eroded the policy space available to central banks and thus curtailed their action. In the South American economies that pursue inflation-targeting policies, central banks started raising monetary policy rates in 2015, especially in the second half of the year. In Mexico, the downtrend in inflation has permitted the authorities to leave the monetary policy rate unchanged.

In countries whose central banks use monetary aggregates as the main policy instrument, the priority still appears to be to stimulate aggregate domestic demand, since the monetary base is growing faster than in 2014. However, not all the countries have been able to prevent a slowdown in the money supply, despite efforts to expand the monetary base.

Generally speaking, average lending rates have remained fairly stable, despite the changes in monetary policy instruments. Credit to the private sector slowed in the Central American and the inflation-targeting economies. In Central America and the English- and Dutch-speaking Caribbean, lending contracted slightly in the first half-year but picked up again in the third quarter. Conversely, in the South American economies whose policy is based on monetary aggregates (which are the exception) lending growth increased in 2015. Analysis of the composition of credit shows a heavy slowdown in lending to industry, whereas consumer lending is the fastest-growing category.

The conditions prevailing on the financial markets have led to depreciation in the currencies of those countries that maintain flexible exchange-rate regimes. The Brazilian real depreciated by 41% against the United States dollar in the first 11 months of 2015, with respect to the prior-year period, while the Colombian peso depreciated by 36.9%, the Mexican peso by 19.4%, the Chilean peso by 14.6%, and the Peruvian nuevo sol by 12%. For many countries, the nominal currency depreciation was large enough to depress the effective exchange rate.

In the first 10 months of 2015 international reserves showed a decline of 3.8% in Latin America and the Caribbean, the largest contraction since the start of the commodity price supercycle that began in 2003. Reserves were down in 22 of the region's economies, and in 13 of these the fall exceeded 5%. The economies with the largest loss of reserves were Argentina (-14.2%), Ecuador (-16.2%), Haiti (-25.1%), Suriname (-36.3%) and the Bolivarian Republic of Venezuela (-31.8%). Conversely, reserves rose in 10 of the region's economies, with the heftiest gains in Costa Rica (9.7%), Jamaica (17.1%) and Saint Lucia (31.3%). The five economies with the region's largest reserves all experienced reserve losses, with the heaviest falls in Chile (-4.6%) and Mexico (-7.0%).

F. Outlook and challenges for 2016

A number of scenarios and possible risks in the global economy in 2016 will unquestionably affect the course of economic activity in the Latin American and Caribbean region. As noted earlier, projections for the next few years are for low global growth, sustained by slow but steady recovery in the developed economies. Serious risks remain, however, which could jeopardize that trajectory. Aside from the eurozone's ongoing difficulties, uncertainty has been mounting over the future performance of China and the emerging economies in general. In the case of China, the most likely scenarios point to continued economic slowdown, with a growth rate of around 6.4% in 2016. Trends in the emerging economies are clouding the aggregate external demand outlook for the countries of Latin America and the Caribbean. To uncertainties over the growth of the global economy is added the lacklustre growth in trade —at 1.5% in 2015, the poorest performance since the crisis of 2007-2009. Global trade volumes are expected to expand at rates of around 2.5% in 2016, still lagging economic growth rates.

Amid slack growth in aggregate global demand and supply-side constraints, raw materials prices are unlikely to recover and will remain at close to end-2015 values. In this context, terms of trade for the Latin American and Caribbean region overall will decline again, although not as steeply as in 2015.

Conditions on the financial markets are expected to toughen with respect to 2015, when emerging economies were already feeling the effects of decreasing availability of financial flows given the uncertainty and volatility that prevailed to a greater or lesser extent for most of the year, along with reduced global liquidity and a gradual rise in the cost of raising funds on the international markets. Accordingly, financial flows to emerging markets, which were down year-on-year in 2015, are unlikely to pick up in 2016. International financial market turbulence is reflecting the effects of possible monetary policy normalization in the United States and the strengthening of the dollar.

As in previous years, global economic trends have strongly differentiated effects on the various countries and subregions of Latin America and the Caribbean, and they tend to sharpen subregional differences in terms of the production and trade bias of the economies. Against a complex and risk-prone external backdrop, 2016 is expected to bring slight positive growth of 0.2% for the region overall, unlike in 2015 —when the regional economy contracted by 0.4%. Central America, including the Spanish-speaking Caribbean and Haiti, is projected to grow by around 4.3% in 2016. The inclusion of Mexico, which is expected at grow at 2.6%, brings that average figure up to 3.0%. South America will post negative growth (-0.8%), essentially reflecting contractions in Brazil (-2.0%) and the Bolivarian Republic of Venezuela (-7.0%). Lastly, the English-speaking Caribbean will register growth of 1.6%.

Domestic demand slowed heavily in 2015, as in 2014, especially private consumption and investment, and will likely continue to do so in 2016, which entails significant risks with respect to future growth capacity.

Stimulating economic growth poses broad challenges for the region. To achieve this, as well as breaking the contractionary investment cycle begun in 2014, the countries would have to increase productivity, which is also lagging heavily by comparison with other regions and with the developed countries. The capacity to increase productivity has been hampered not only by the drop in investment, but also by the weakening of the region's industrial and manufacturing sectors over the past few years. This weakening has gone hand in hand with increasing deterioration in the labour markets, which are showing rising employment in informal, low-productivity sectors. In a context of slack economic growth, the region must also find ways to safeguard the social progress made over recent years.

Amid declining fiscal revenues, which have set off an entrenchment of the public accounts, it becomes all the more essential to establish fiscal rules to prioritize capital spending. As ECLAC has argued before, it is extremely important to establish countercyclical investment protection regimes in order to stand up to the region's macroeconomic volatility. Regimes that complement countercyclical policies with measures to protect (and stimulate) investment at the bottom of the cycle can be much more effective than fiscal rules based solely on spending or deficit targets when it comes to minimizing adjustment costs and boosting expectations of potential growth and future stability.

Chapter I

Global economic trends

The world economy grew by 2.4% in 2015, two tenths of a percentage point less than in 2014, while in 2016 there is expected to be a recovery to 2.9% sustained by both developed and developing countries, with China the exception

World economic growth slowed from 2.6% in 2014 to 2.4% in 2015, a drop of 0.2 percentage points. Underlying this outcome was the slowdown in developing economies, where growth declined from 4.3% in 2014 to 3.8% in 2015, and particularly China, which grew by less than 7% for the first time since 1990 (6.8% in 2015).

The developed countries, conversely, while still expanding much more slowly than the developing world, have picked up speed in recent years, with growth there rising from 1.7% in 2014 to 1.9% in 2015.

Projections for 2016, while indicating a better performance than in 2015, have been subject to downward revisions. The expectation for the year is that the global growth rate will pick up by 0.5 percentage points to 2.9%, with both developed and developing countries accelerating. The growth rate should rise by three tenths of a percentage point to 2.2% in the developed countries and by five tenths to 4.3% in developing ones. China is naturally an outlier, as its economy has been moving in the opposite direction to the other subregions' and growth there is expected to slow to 6.4% (see figure I.1).

Figure I.1
Selected regions and countries: gross domestic product growth, 2013-2016
(Percentages)

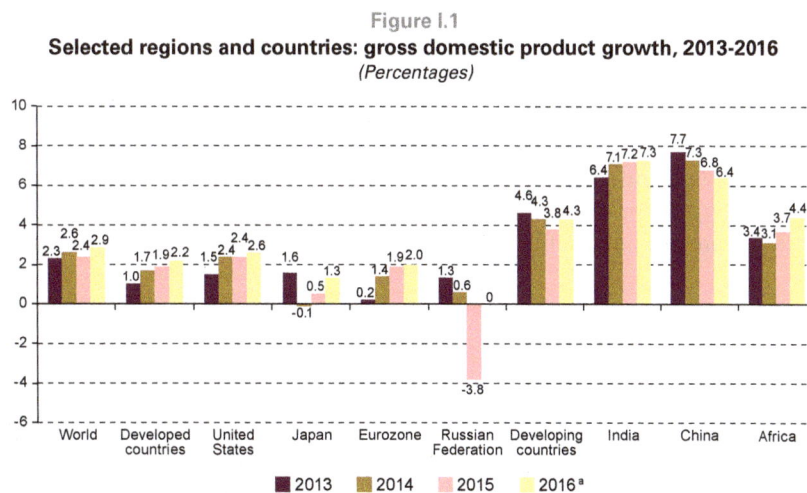

Source: Economic Commission for Latin America and the Caribbean (ECLAC), on the basis of United Nations, *World Economic Situation and Prospects, 2016*, New York, December 2015.
[a] The figures for 2016 are projections.

Commodity prices fell sharply in 2015 and are not expected to recover significantly in 2016

The hint of a recovery in commodity prices in the second quarter of 2015 did not last, as they began to fall substantially once again from July. An undoubted factor was uncertainty about the situation in China, which will be discussed further on. This came to a head in June, when the stock market began to collapse, and in August, with the sudden devaluation of the country's currency.

Metal and agricultural commodity prices have been trending steadily downward for five years, since early 2011. After declines of 11% and 6%, respectively, in 2014, the downward trend intensified in 2015, especially for metals, whose prices fell by 21%, while agricultural commodity prices dropped by 10%.

The cumulative declines between January 2011 and October 2015 totalled almost 50% for metals and 30% for agricultural commodities. The energy group (comprising oil, natural gas and coal) experienced the largest decline in the commodities category in 2015, with prices dropping by 24% between January and October. The cumulative decline between January 2011 and October 2015 was almost 50%, matching that for metals (see figure I.2). Crude oil was the worst performer in this group, as a cumulative decline of 57% between January 2011 and late November 2015 took its price back down to levels not seen since the 2008-2009 global crisis.

Figure I.2
International commodity prices, January 2011 to October 2015
(Index: January 2011=100)

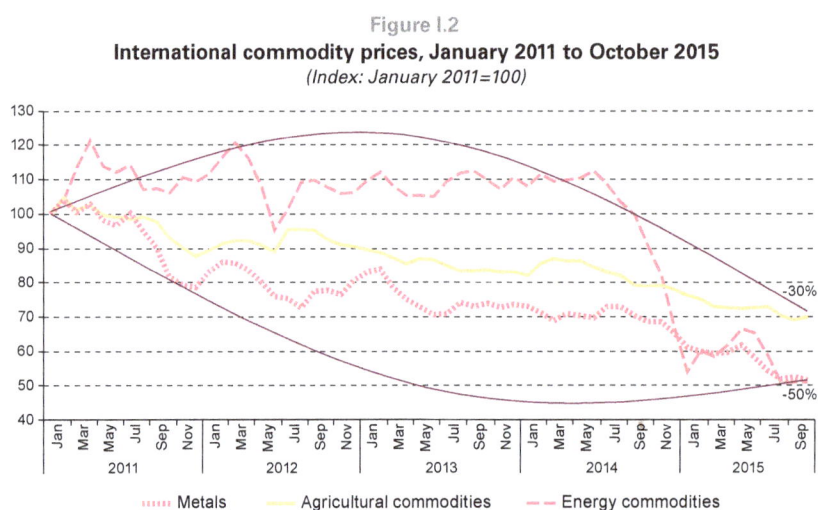

Source: Economic Commission for Latin America and the Caribbean (ECLAC), on the basis of World Bank Commodity Price Data (Pink Sheet).

This downward cycle in commodity prices has been due to a number of factors, as has been much discussed. First, global supply has grown because of increased investment in natural resource sectors during the price boom of the last decade. Second, demand has slackened, mainly because of lower growth in the Chinese economy. The shift in China's growth strategy from an essentially investment-based (and commodity-intensive) model to one relying on domestic consumption and services has resulted in lower demand for raw materials, especially industrial ones such as metals and energy commodities. Thus, while the rebalancing of demand towards consumption has progressed slowly so far, there are no grounds for expecting Chinese demand for these commodities to be very dynamic in future.

An additional factor in commodity price behaviour over recent years needs to be considered, namely the increasing role played by commodities as financial assets, meaning that their prices have also been driven by expectations of future conditions in the market and by speculative factors that are difficult to predict.

For 2016, a number of considerations suggest that any recovery in commodity prices will be small, and consequently that annual price changes relative to 2015 averages will continue to be negative. In the oil market, the members of the Organization of Petroleum Exporting Countries (OPEC) have raised their crude production quota despite the excess supply seen during 2015, thus considerably expanding stocks. In addition, the lifting of the sanctions placed on the Islamic Republic of Iran because of its nuclear programme will have a significant impact on the global oil supply.

On the demand side, global consumption is expected to rise by just 1% during 2016.[1] These factors are expected to keep the oil price in 2016 at levels similar to those of late 2015, implying a further fall of about 5% in the average price for 2016 relative to the 2015 average.

Prices in the metals markets can be expected to continue falling in 2016 since, while lower prices have led to a drop in investment in the sector, a longer period will be required for supply to adjust to weaker demand.

Where agricultural commodities are concerned, lastly, production continued to grow during the third quarter of 2015 despite apprehension about the effects of the El Niño climate phenomenon, with price declines persisting as a result. Nonetheless, they have suffered the smallest cumulative price fall of any commodity group since the beginning of the downward cycle (30%), and they also look set to benefit most from the change in the Chinese growth model to one based on consumption.[2]

World trade showed signs of a sharp slowdown

World trade grew by just 1.5% in volume during the first nine months of 2015 relative to the same period the year before, this being the lowest rate of increase in the period since the global crisis (see figure I.3).

Figure I.3
World: trade volume growth, 2009-2015
(Percentages)

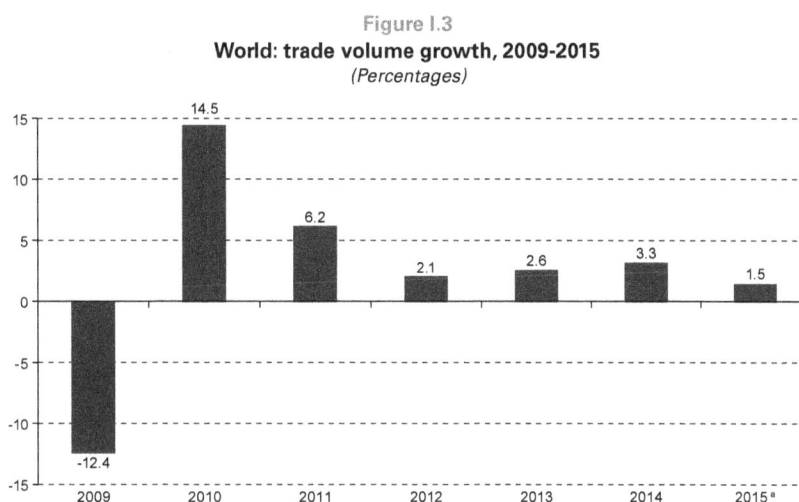

Source: Economic Commission for Latin America and the Caribbean (ECLAC), on the basis of figures from the Netherlands Bureau of Economic Policy Analysis (CPB).
ª The 2015 figure is the cumulative value between January and September (the latest available) relative to the same period the year before.

This weakness was due essentially to low volumes of exports from the United States, showing the effects of dollar appreciation, and from the emerging economies of Asia, whose export volumes have suffered despite their currencies depreciating. In the eurozone, meanwhile, a large currency depreciation has gone together with positive year-on-year export volume growth. The same has happened in Japan, where export volume growth rates have been positive, albeit steadily declining.

Given expectations of an upturn in global economic activity encompassing both developed and emerging countries (although not China), it would be natural to expect the slowdown in trade volume growth to come to a halt in 2016.

An important development for world trade was the successful conclusion of the Trans-Pacific Partnership (TPP) negotiations in October 2015. This will be the world's largest free trade area, comprising 12 countries that between them account for almost 40% of global GDP (in current dollars), 23% of world goods exports and 26% of imports.[3]

---

[1] OPEC, OPEC Monthly Oil Market Report, 12 November 2015 [online] http://www.opec.org/opec_web/static_files_project/media/downloads/publications/MOMR_November_2015.pdf.

[2] According to ECLAC, "over the coming decades, China is expected to sharply increase its imports of a wide range of raw and processed food products, such as palm oil, sugar, meat, dairy, processed and unprocessed cereals, fruit, coffee and legumes" (ECLAC, Latin America and the Caribbean in the World Economy (LC/G.2650-P), Santiago, 2015, p. 61).

[3] The 12 countries are Australia, Brunei Darussalam, Canada, Chile, Japan, Malaysia, Mexico, New Zealand, Peru, Singapore, the United States and Viet Nam. The group includes 5 of the world's 20 largest economies (ECLAC, 2015, op. cit., p. 39).

However, the TPP cannot be expected to affect world trade dynamism substantially in the short run, as it is not likely to come into force until 2017 (following ratification by the parliaments of the participating countries during 2016).

The volatility characterizing financial markets during 2015 intensified in the second half of the year because of financial developments in China

On 13 June, share prices on the Chinese stock market began a decline that would almost completely reverse the large gains seen since the beginning of the year. Although the Chinese central bank and the capital market regulator reacted with a series of measures, they were unable to increase confidence. In early August, in an effort to stimulate economic activity, and in the wake of discouraging news on exports, the People's Bank of China took the unexpected decision to change the rules used to set the exchange rate of the country's currency: the midpoint around which the yuan could fluctuate would be determined by the previous day's closing price rather than being set by the bank as hitherto. The result was that the yuan depreciated by 3% in two days and the exchange rate experienced its largest daily fluctuations since the early 1990s.[4] In addition, there were large capital outflows from China that were not stemmed until October 2015.

The events in China had a large impact on global financial markets. Stock exchanges suffered major losses in parallel with China's. In a particularly testing period of just six business days (from 18 to 25 August), the Chinese stock market fell by 27%, the Nikkei index in Japan by 14%, the stock exchange of Hong Kong Special Administrative Region of China by 13%, the S&P index in the United States by 11% and the European SXXP index by 11%.

In the same period, indicators of market volatility ("fear indices") jumped (see figure I.4) and currencies regarded as safe havens (among them the euro, the yen and the Swiss franc) appreciated strongly (by 5% in six days in all three cases), showing that investors were seeking refuge.

Figure I.4
Implied market volatility indices [a], January 2014 to November 2015

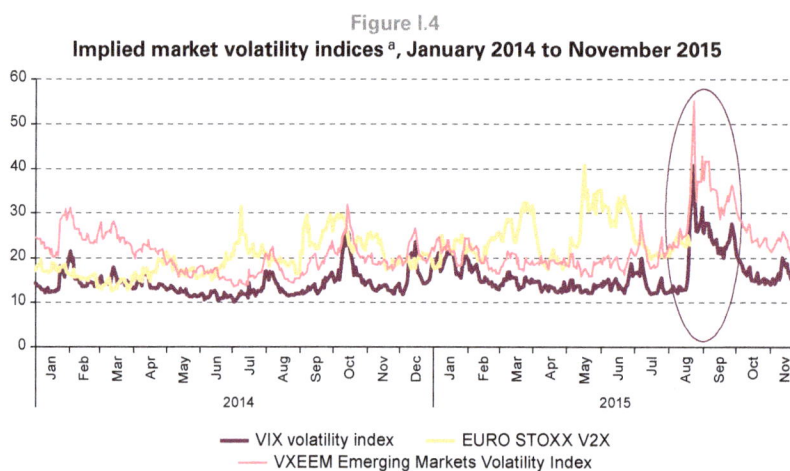

Source: Economic Commission for Latin America and the Caribbean (ECLAC), on the basis of Bloomberg.
[a] VIX is prepared by the Chicago Board Options Exchange (CBOE) from S&P 500 call and put option prices, and measures expected volatility over the next 30 days. Following the same logic, the CBOE also produces the VXEEM index, which measures volatility in emerging markets, while Deutsche Börse and Goldman Sachs produce the V2X index, which measures eurozone volatility.

The remaining Asian currencies (including the Thai baht, the Indian rupee, the Korean won and the Malaysian ringgit) depreciated substantially in parallel with the Chinese currency, although this decline actually began in mid-year, coinciding with the start of the Chinese stock market crash.

The decision by the United States Federal Reserve not to raise the federal funds rate at its meeting of mid-September 2015 did nothing to reduce the prevailing uncertainty in the markets, as these interpreted its inaction on rates as a lack of confidence in the world economy, so that the decision was not necessarily perceived as good news.

---

4   The official reason given for devaluing the Chinese currency, however, was to move to a more market-based exchange-rate regime so that the yuan would be accepted by the International Monetary Fund (IMF) as part of its basket of reserve currencies on a par with the United States dollar, the euro, the yen and the pound sterling.

A degree of calm returned to the markets towards the year's end (see figures I.1, I.2, I.3 and I.4). In fact, most financial indicators turned up quite strongly during October. Positive figures have also come out for the United States domestic economy, so that by late November the market was placing high odds (72%) on the Federal Reserve raising interest rates at its meeting of 15 and 16 December 2015. If there is a rise, it will be the first since 2006, following six years of near-zero rates.

A number of risk factors will remain in 2016, including the health of the Chinese economy and the likelihood that there will be less financing available for emerging markets

Given the size of the Chinese economy and its importance for global economic activity, world trade and the demand for raw materials, one continuing risk lies in the health of that economy and the question of whether it might slow more than forecast.[5]

This uncertainty will be compounded in 2016 by the impact on financial markets of what has been called interest rate "lift-off" by the United States Federal Reserve. Although the markets have already factored increases in and these are expected to be gradual and not too disruptive, there will still be consequences in future for the relative attractiveness of investments in currencies other than the dollar.

One expectation, then, must be that financial flows to emerging markets (including Latin America) will decrease, the prices of their financial assets will drop and their currencies will depreciate, especially in the case of the economies perceived as riskiest by the markets.

The central banks of the countries whose currencies depreciate most quickly will be faced with a rather intractable policy dilemma; they will feel constrained to raise interest rates to contain the increased inflationary pressures resulting from this greater depreciation, but will have to try not to trammel economic recovery in the process.

At the same time, the cost of financing in international markets is likely to begin rising gradually as United States interest rates increase. This will naturally mean higher debt service costs and thus risks for the private sectors of several countries that increased leverage during the long period of low-cost borrowing.[6] Although this change has been well flagged, meaning there has been time to restructure such debt, it is likely that not all agents have been able to reduce this vulnerability.

Emerging economies were already suffering from reduced availability of financial flows in 2015, given the uncertainty and volatility that prevailed to a greater or lesser degree throughout the year. According to the monthly indicator of portfolio capital flows prepared by the Institute of International Finance (IIF), cumulative annual flows into emerging economies were 65% lower in October 2015 than a year earlier.

There can be no expectation of a recovery in the financing flows available for emerging markets in 2016, given the reduction in global liquidity that will follow the normalization of monetary conditions in the United States and a degree of ongoing risk aversion in the face of uncertainty on several fronts.

---

[5]   In 2014, China represented 14% of global GDP and 11% of world trade. In addition, it used 11% of the world's crude oil and was the largest consumer of most of the major metals and minerals, accounting for over 50% of total demand for iron, aluminium, copper and nickel.

[6]   See International Monetary Fund (IMF), *World Economic Outlook (WEO). Adjusting to Lower Commodity Prices*, October 2015, chap. 3 [online] http://www.imf.org/external/pubs/ft/weo/2015/02/.

Chapter II

The external sector

Commodity prices continued to weaken in the second half of the year, adversely affecting the region's terms of trade

The sharp falls in commodity prices across the world —analysed in chapter I "Global economic trends"— were reflected in the average prices at which Latin America and Caribbean countries export those products. Given that 44% of the region's exports are commodities, the drop in the prices of most of these products has a major effect on its export prices. Table II.1 shows the variations in the Latin American export commodity price index,[7] with the general index dropping by 30% from its 2014 level. Oil has led this fall, losing 48%, followed by minerals and metals, where prices fell by 23%, and agricultural products, whose prices were down by 15%.

Commodity prices are expected to fall again in 2016, although less steeply than in the current year, so the prices of Latin American and Caribbean commodity exports can be expected to deteriorate slightly overall (see table II.1).[8]

Table II.1
Latin America: annual variation in the export commodity price index, 2015 [a] and 2016 [b]
(Percentages)

	2015	2016
Agricultural products	-15	-2
Food, tropical beverages and oilseed products	-17	-3
Food	-13	-3
Tropical beverages	-20	-4
Oils and oilseed products	-22	-1
Forestry and agricultural raw materials	-4	1
Minerals and metals	-23	-5
Energy	-44	-5
Crude oil	-48	-5
Derivatives	-36	-8
Coal	-17	3
Natural gas	-40	-2
Total commodities	-30	-4
Total commodities excluding energy	-19	-2

Source: Economic Commission for Latin America and the Caribbean (ECLAC), on the basis of figures provided by Bloomberg, the World Bank, the International Monetary Fund (IMF) and The Economist Intelligence Unit.
[a] Estimates.
[b] Projections.

---

[7] ECLAC constructs this index of the region's export commodity prices, with product groups weighted by their share in the regional export basket.
[8] Because, even if current levels were to recover somewhat, this would generally not be sufficient to achieve a positive change in the average indices for 2016 from their 2015 levels.

The impact of lower commodity prices on each country's terms of trade varies according to the weighting of the different products in their individual export and import baskets. For the region as a whole, the terms of trade are estimated to have deteriorated by 9% in 2015, making this the fourth consecutive year of deterioration (see figure II.1).

Figure II.1
Latin America and the Caribbean (selected countries and country groupings):
rate of variation in the terms of trade, 2012-2016 [a]
(Percentages)

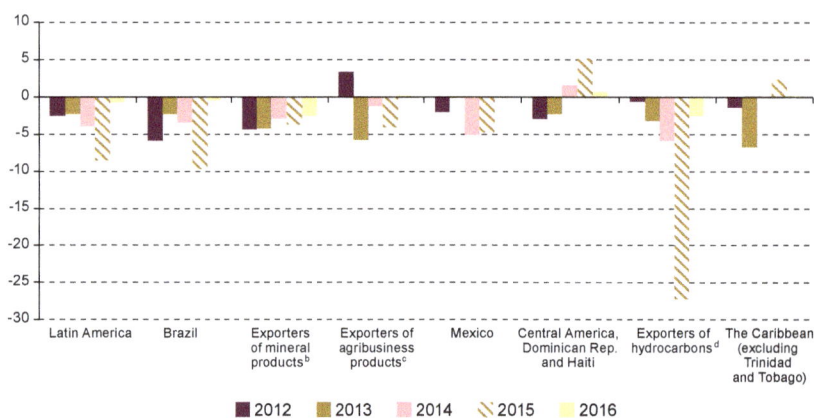

Legend: ■ 2012 ■ 2013 ■ 2014 ⧅ 2015 ■ 2016

Source: Economic Commission for Latin America and the Caribbean (ECLAC), on the basis of official figures.
[a] The figures for 2015 and 2016 are estimates and projections, respectively.
[b] Chile and Peru.
[c] Argentina, Paraguay and Uruguay.
[d] Bolivarian Republic of Venezuela, Colombia, Ecuador, Plurinational State of Bolivia and Trinidad and Tobago.

The Central American countries, along with the Dominican Republic and Haiti, benefited from the fall in the prices of energy products, of which they are large net importers. For this group, the terms of trade improved by 5%. The same happened in the Caribbean food- and fuel-importing countries (generally all Caribbean countries apart from Trinidad and Tobago), where the terms of trade rose by 2% in 2015.

In contrast, the countries worst affected by the trend of foreign trade prices during the year were those whose exports are mainly concentrated in hydrocarbons (Bolivarian Republic of Venezuela, Colombia, Ecuador, Plurinational State of Bolivia, and Trinidad and Tobago), because their terms of trade fell by 27% in 2015. In Brazil, the terms of trade declined by 10%, since its export basket is heavily weighted with certain products whose prices fell by a large amount this year (metals, particularly iron, which plummeted by around 42% in 2015; and foods such as soybeans and sugar, whose prices fell by over 20%). In Mexico, the terms of trade fell by 5%: although this country mainly exports manufactures to the United States market, it is also a net crude oil exporter, so its export prices have suffered a major shock. In countries whose exports are concentrated in minerals and metals, and also in the group that exports agribusiness products, the terms of trade declined by 4%. In several of these countries, lower export prices were partly offset by a reduction in the prices of their energy product imports, so the terms-of-trade deterioration was mitigated.

Aside from terms-of-trade movements in the different countries and subregions, it is worth quantifying the monetary losses or gains caused by the differential trend of the countries' import and export prices between 2014 and 2015. In the latter year, these losses amounted to nearly US$ 92 billion, equivalent to 1.9% of regional GDP.[9] At the country grouping level, the largest losses occurred in hydrocarbon-exporting economies (with losses equivalent to 4% of their GDP). In contrast, the group consisting of Central America, Dominican Republic and Haiti gained from the export and import price trends by an amount equivalent to 2.4% of their GDP.

---

9 These losses exclusively represent the effect of the differential trend of import and export prices on the trade balance. For the calculation methodology, see ECLAC, *Economic Survey of Latin America and the Caribbean, 2015* (LC/G.2645-P), Santiago, 2015.

Given the expected future path of export commodity prices, the terms of trade for Latin America as a whole look set to decline further in 2016, although the fall will be much less steep than in the current year. No major changes are expected in the terms of trade in any subregion in the coming year; and in the case of metals- and hydrocarbon-exporting countries, the terms of trade are likely to decline more moderately than in 2015 (see figure II.1).

Despite the worsening the trade balance, the balance-of-payments current account deficit narrowed in nominal terms

The region's balance-of-payments current account deficit improved in 2015 in nominal terms, narrowing from US$ 175 billion to US$ 169.5 billion. This improvement was offset by the reduction in regional GDP measured in dollars, however, so the current account deficit as a percentage of GDP widened in 2015 to 3.5%, four percentage points larger than the gap recorded in the previous year (see figure II.2).

Figure II.2
Latin America (19 countries): balance-of-payments current account by component, 2005-2015
(Percentages of GDP)

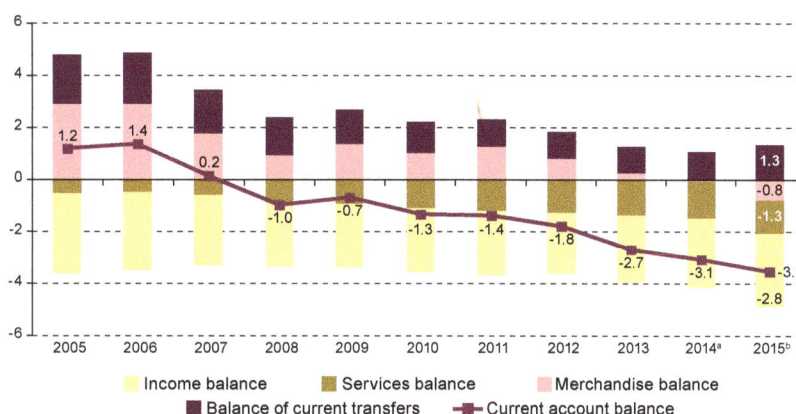

Source: Economic Commission for Latin America and the Caribbean (ECLAC), on the basis of official figures.
[a] The 2014 figures for the Bolivarian Republic of Venezuela are estimates.
[b] The 2015 figures are projections.

Among the components of the current account, the merchandise trade balance worsened very significantly from a deficit of US$ 4 billion in 2014 to a gap of US$ 38.2 billion in 2015. This is the second consecutive year in which this account has been in deficit, a situation not seen since 2001. This worsening of the merchandise trade balance reflected a sharp fall in the value of the region's exports (down by 14% in 2015), and a decline in import values, the absolute magnitude of which was insufficient to compensate for the 10% drop in exports in 2015.

The latter is basically explained by the 15% fall in Latin American export prices. The decrease in export value reflected a 7% drop in prices, owing mainly to energy products, and a 3% shrinking in volumes, given the moderate level of activity in several of the region's economies (see figure II.3).

Figure II.3

**Latin America (selected country groupings): rate of change
in international trade, by volume and prices, 2015 [a]**

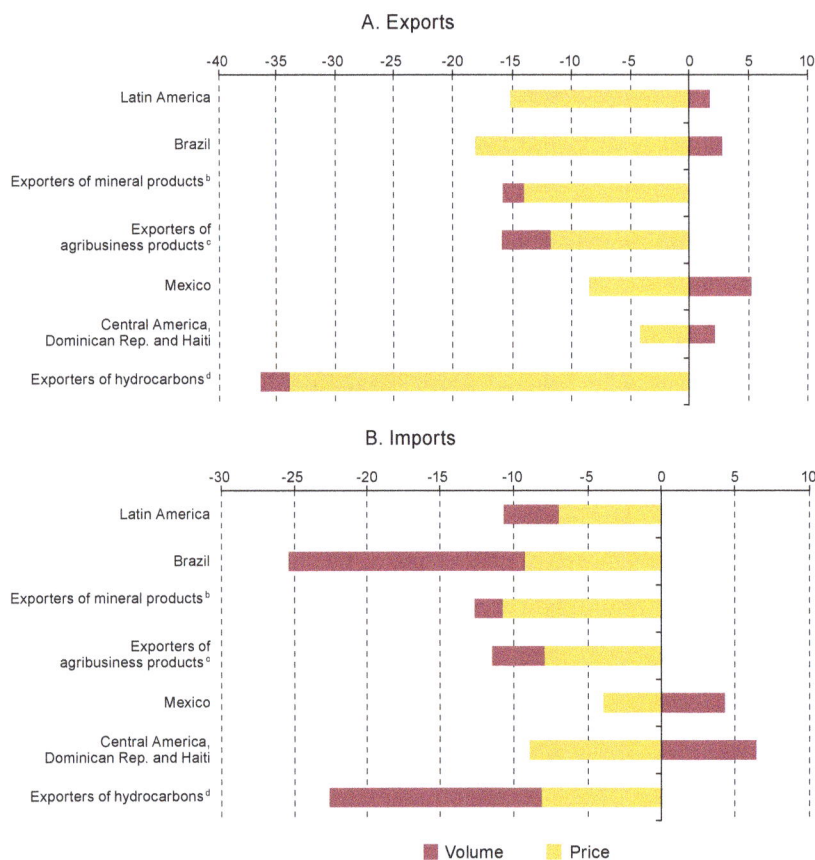

(Percentages)

A. Exports

B. Imports

■ Volume   ■ Price

Source: Economic Commission for Latin America and the Caribbean (ECLAC) on the basis of official figures.
[a] The figures shown are estimates.
[b] Chile and Peru.
[c] Argentina, Paraguay and Uruguay.
[d] Bolivarian Republic of Venezuela, Colombia, Ecuador, Plurinational State of Bolivia and Trinidad and Tobago.

The balance of trade in services improved significantly, from a deficit of US$ 80.9 billion in 2014 to a deficit of US$ 60.4 billion in 2015. This improvement on the 2014 result is mainly due to a reduction in imports of transport services, associated with smaller imports of the goods mentioned above. There were also smaller outgoings on the travel account as a result of depreciations in several of the region's currencies. The other services as a whole contracted, as a result of the region's lower activity rate during the year, which has contributed to a reduction in net outflows on the travel account.

The current transfers account reported its customary surplus in 2015, actually improving on the previous year's performance from US$ 62.6 billion in 2014 to US$ 64.6 billion in 2015. This increase was mainly due to the positive trend of migrant remittances, which is the main component of the current transfer category. Remittances are a very important source of financing for several of the region's countries, including El Salvador, Guatemala, Haiti, Honduras, Nicaragua, and others. In 2015, according to the most recent data available, migrant remittances have grown by 6% on average in relation to the previous year.[10] The improvement in the labour market in the United States was reflected in an increase in remittances to Mexico (5% in the first 10 months, compared with the year-earlier period) and to several Central American countries (11% in the case of Guatemala and 9% in Honduras over the same period). In these countries, remittances gave a significant boost to domestic demand and, thus, also played a substantial role in the growth of import volumes.

---

[10]   The figures represent the cumulative amount for 2015 up to the month for which each country possesses information.

The South American countries that receive the largest amount of remittances from Spain (Colombia, Ecuador, Paraguay and Plurinational State of Bolivia) displayed mixed results, with growth of 1% in the Plurinational State of Bolivia and 14% in Colombia, but a 9% fall in the case of Ecuador (see figure II.4), mainly as a result of the depreciation of the euro against the dollar (the latter being the currency in which remittances are expressed).

Figure II.4

Latin America and the Caribbean (13 countries): variation in inflows of remittances from migrants abroad, 2012-2015 [a]

(Percentages)

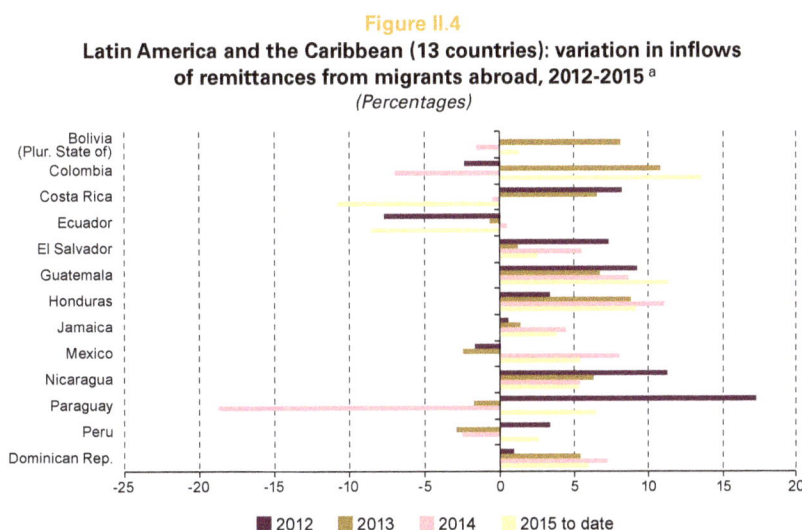

Source: Economic Commission for Latin America and the Caribbean (ECLAC) on the basis of official figures.
[a] The figures for 2015 represent the cumulative annual total up to October for Colombia, El Salvador, Guatemala, Honduras, Mexico and Nicaragua; up to September for Paraguay and Peru, up to July for Jamaica and the Plurinational State of Bolivia, and up to June for Costa Rica, the Dominican Republic and Ecuador.

Lastly, as shown in figure II.2, the income account has the largest deficit on the current account and generates the largest outflows of net funds abroad for the region. The main component of this account consists of profit repatriation by foreign direct investment firms to their parent companies abroad (these outflows represent an average of nearly 70% of the income account); but they also include external debt interest, among other items.

In 2015, the income account improved by over US$ 19.3 billion, from a deficit of US$ 154.8 billion in 2014 to one of US$ 135.5 billion this year. This is mainly due to the reduction in outflows of funds representing profit repatriation. The negative trend of the region's export prices, in line with the deterioration of commodity prices, eroded the earnings of transnational enterprises established in the region; and, as a result, also reduced the proportion of firms repatriating profits to their parent companies.

The financial flows received by the region in 2015 were not sufficient to cover the balance-of-payments current account deficit, and international reserves had to be drawn down to bridge the gap

In 2015, financial flows to emerging countries as a whole declined, owing to the uncertainty and volatility prevailing on the financial markets throughout the year.[11] Latin America was not immune to this reality, and, in 2015, the net inflow of financial resources to the region, in other words the balance of the capital and financial accounts of the balance of payments) totalled 2.8% of GDP, which was insufficient to fully finance the 3% of GDP current account deficit. As a result, the region as a whole used international reserves amounting to 0.7% of GDP to cover the shortfall.[12]

Within the financial account there were a number of interesting trends,[13] for example, the behaviour of net foreign direct investment (FDI) which is the main financial flow for the region as a whole and amounted in 2014 to

---

[11] In the first half of 2015, the situation in Greece was a factor contributing to market instability, whereas the second half of the year felt the impact of the financial events in China (see chapter I, "Global economic trends").

[12] The balance of the capital and financial account mentioned includes the balance-of-payments category "Errors and omissions".

[13] Financial account information is available up to the third quarter of 2015 for four countries whose capital flows accounted for 80% of the regional total in 2014, and whose economies are large or financially open: Brazil, Chile, Mexico and Peru.

around US$ 137 billion.[14] In 2015, the net inflow fell by around 22% from the previous year's level. Although the investments of trans-Latin enterprises abroad declined, those of multinationals in the region contracted more sharply, which resulted in a decrease in net flows of this type of investment. As there is nothing to suggest that the last quarter of the year will differ greatly from the previous three, this rate of variation can be assumed for the full year, so net direct investment will close at around US$ 107 billion.

Net regional inflows of portfolio capital —basically investments in bonds and shares— also retreated sharply from the year-earlier levels. In 2014, these flows had attained just over US$ 115 billion, and a 40% fall is expected for 2015, so they are likely to close the year at around US$ 70 billion.

Although Brazil and Chile saw a repatriation of assets from abroad (in Chile, these mainly involved pension funds bringing capital back into the country), the amount in question was insufficient to offset portfolio outflows reflecting reduced purchases of shares and Latin American debt by foreign investors (which dropped to half of their 2014 level). This was largely due to the reduction in liabilities of Brazilian external debt, which have fallen by nearly 70% year-on-year in the first three quarters of 2015 —a situation which, as will be seen, is closely related to developments on the primary external debt securities issuance markets.

Latin America and Caribbean debt issues on international markets fell substantially in 2015, a situation that became more pronounced in the second half of the year

As shown by the data on balance-of-payments financial flows, primary issues on international debt markets declined substantially in 2015 (by a cumulative 40% from January to November 2015, compared with the year-earlier period). The reduced access to international bond markets became more acute in the second half of the year: in the third quarter, total issues were just US$ 10 billion, 63% down from the same period in 2014, and the lowest quarterly level since June 2009 when the global financial crisis was in full swing.

Considering cumulative issues over 12 months at the sector level, the year-on-year reductions recorded as of November amount to 75% for the banks, 48% for the private sector, 46% for quasi-sovereigns, 13% for sovereigns, and 7% for supranationals (see figure II.5).[15]

Figure II.5
Latin America and the Caribbean: annual variation in cumulative debt issues on international markets over the last 12 months by institutional sector, January 2014 to October 2015
(Percentages)

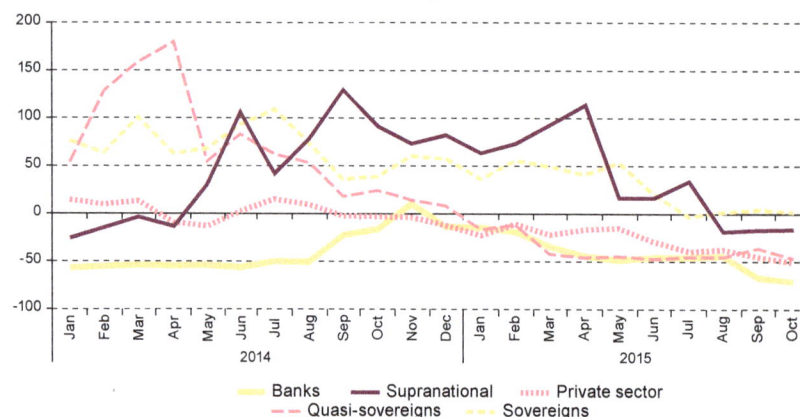

Source: Economic Commission for Latin America and the Caribbean (ECLAC) on the basis of figures obtained from the Latin Finance Bonds Database.

---

[14] Wherever possible the figures used are aligned to the sixth edition of the Balance of Payments Manual published by the International Monetary Fund (IMF). For other countries, the data reflect the fifth edition of the Manual. The Bolivarian Republic of Venezuela is not included, because it does not yet have complete information for 2014.

[15] The quasi-sovereign sector includes public development banks or State enterprises, among other entities. The supranational sector includes regional development banks, such as the Latin American Development Bank (CAF) or the Central American Bank for Economic Integration (CABEI).

A large part of the fall is explained by the case of Brazil, where issues are declining at a rate of 80% year-on-year. This is consistent with the pattern observed in the balance of payments, where the most affected account in Brazil, as noted, was the portfolio capital account, and particularly the purchase of debt securities by foreign investors. The Brazilian quasi- sovereign sector borrowed heavily in 2014, with the State oil company, Petrobras, alone issuing nearly US$ 14 billion of debt in the first quarter of the year. Nonetheless, owing to the well-known problems in which it became involved, Petrobras issued just US$ 2.5 billion in the whole of 2015.

The region's average sovereign risk rose moderately in 2015, with country risk rising most markedly in Ecuador, the Bolivarian Republic of Venezuela and Brazil

The region's average sovereign risk spread, measured by the Emerging Market Bond Index Global (EMBIG), rose by 53 basis points between January and November 2014, to reach a level of 561 basis points on the latter date. Ecuador, Brazil and the Bolivarian Republic of Venezuela are the three countries for which country risk rose by most in the year to November (324, 180 and 148 basis points, respectively) (see figure II.6).

Figure II.6
Latin America (15 countries): variation in sovereign risk according to the Emerging Market Bond Index Global (EMBIG), 2014 and 2015
(Basis points)

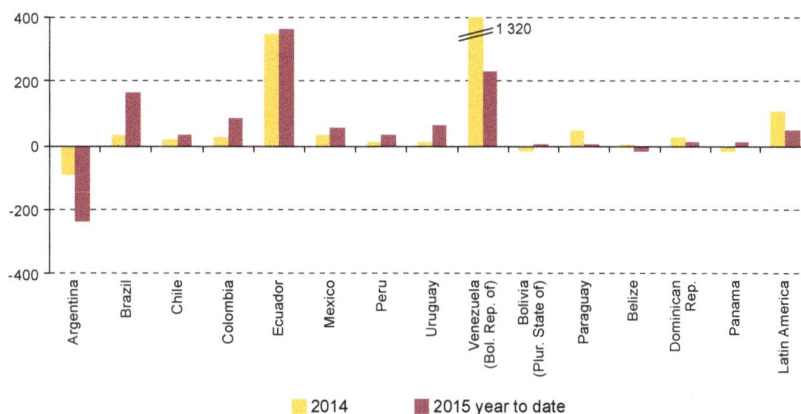

■ 2014   ■ 2015 year to date

Source: Economic Commission for Latin America and the Caribbean (ECLAC), on the basis of figures from the Latin Finance Bonds Database, JP Morgan and Merrill Lynch.

Panama, Peru and Chile are the countries in the region where the sovereign risk rating is lowest at the present time (spreads of just over 200 basis points in all three cases). These are followed by the Plurinational State of Bolivia, Uruguay, Mexico and Colombia, all below 300 points. Brazil and Argentina represent the next group, with spreads of over 400 basis points; then, far behind are Ecuador (1,207 basis points) and the Bolivarian Republic of Venezuela (2,605 basis points).

As noted in chapter I, the downward trend in financial flows to emerging markets is expected to continue in 2016, compared with previous years. This reflects the reduced global liquidity available following the normalization of monetary conditions in the United States, and the persistence of a degree of risk aversion, stemming from the uncertainty prevailing on several fronts. In the particular case of Latin America, this situation will naturally vary between countries, and some will suffer more constraints than others in access to financing.

Should the situation in China, or the perception thereof, worsen, higher risk-aversion scenarios could arise, along with a flight to quality, as occurred in August 2015 with a surge in demand for currencies considered a safe haven (particularly the yen, the Swiss franc and the euro, in addition to the dollar). Naturally, this would further weaken financing flows to emerging countries.

In the case of Latin America and the Caribbean, the above is compounded by the fact that the region is less attractive for foreign capital as a result of the slower economic growth or even contraction recorded in 2015; and, in several countries, the poor prospects for export prices, which look set to continue in the medium term. In Central America, however, given its looser financial integration with international markets, the effect of the normalization of monetary conditions in the United States ought to be felt less than in the more financially integrated countries of South America or, of course, Mexico.

Chapter III

Economic activity

Economic activity contracted by 0.4% in Latin America and the Caribbean in 2015, as the slowdown begun in 2011 took hold

The Latin American and Caribbean region's gross domestic product (GDP) shrank by 0.4% in 2015, which translated into a 1.5% downturn in per capita GDP. This performance, the poorest since 2009, left no doubt that the growth slowdown evident in the region over the past five years has sharpened (see figure III.1).

Figure III.1
Latin America and the Caribbean (selected countries and groupings): contribution to regional GDP growth, 2008-2015
(Percentages on the basis of dollars at constant 2010 prices)

A. Latin America and the Caribbean

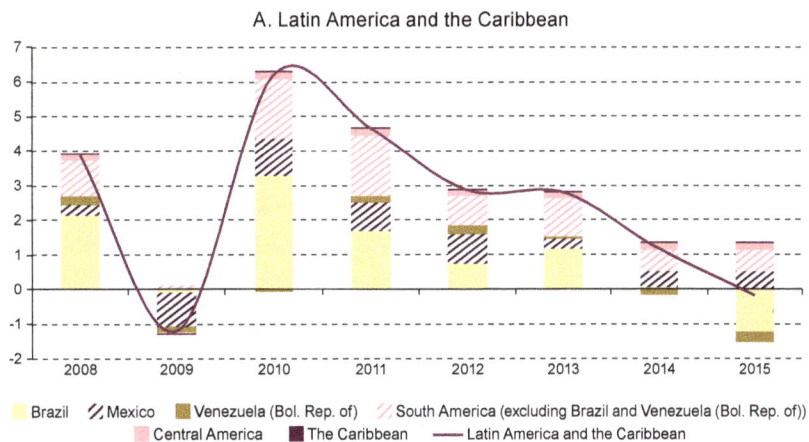

Brazil   Mexico   Venezuela (Bol. Rep. of)   South America (excluding Brazil and Venezuela (Bol. Rep. of))
Central America   The Caribbean   — Latin America and the Caribbean

Figure III.1 (concluded)

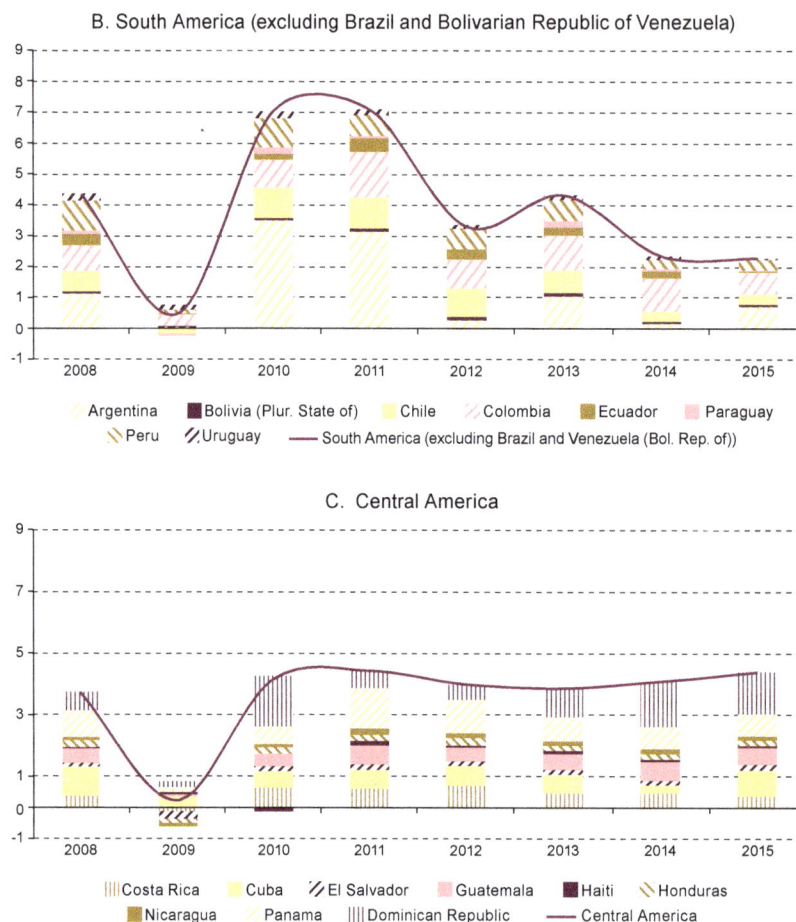

B. South America (excluding Brazil and Bolivarian Republic of Venezuela)

Legend:
Argentina · Bolivia (Plur. State of) · Chile · Colombia · Ecuador · Paraguay · Peru · Uruguay · — South America (excluding Brazil and Venezuela (Bol. Rep. of))

C. Central America

Legend:
Costa Rica · Cuba · El Salvador · Guatemala · Haiti · Honduras · Nicaragua · Panama · Dominican Republic · — Central America

Source: Economic Commission for Latin America and the Caribbean (ECLAC), on the basis of official figures.

The shrinking economic activity at the regional level reflected the downturn in the South American economies, which, as a group, went from growth of 0.6% in 2014 to contraction of 1.6% in 2015. The subregion's performance was heavily influenced by the negative growth posted by Brazil and the Bolivarian Republic of Venezuela in 2015.

The English- and Dutch-speaking Caribbean economies experienced a small uptick in growth, from 0.7% in 2014 to 1.0% in 2015, despite the impacts of natural disasters on some of these countries. Dominica, by contrast, suffered severe enough effects to produce an outright contraction in GDP in 2015.

Economic activity gained momentum in the Central American economies and Mexico in 2015. The growth rate picked up from 4.0% in 2014 to 4.4% in 2015 in Central America, and from 2.2% to 2.5% in Mexico (see figure III.1).

In terms of subregions, the South American economies' contribution to the growth of the region overall has been shrinking since 2011, although it has held steady for the last three years if Brazil and the Bolivarian Republic of Venezuela are excluded from the estimates. Both Central America and the English- and Dutch-speaking Caribbean have seen their contribution to growth increase. The contribution of Brazil and the Bolivarian Republic of Venezuela has turned negative.

Private consumption and gross fixed capital formation made a negative contribution to GDP growth in 2015

In regional terms, domestic demand was down by 0.7% in 2015, with a downturn in private consumption (-0.3%) and in gross fixed capital formation (-4.2%) and a marginal gain in public consumption (0.7%). The negative contribution of private consumption to GDP growth in the region —which had not occurred since the international financial crisis of 2009— began in the second quarter of 2015 and will likely intensify in the third and fourth quarters. What is more, gross fixed capital formation in Latin America appears to have shrunk throughout 2015, running up seven straight quarters of contraction (see figure III.2).

Figure III.2
Latin America: GDP variation and contribution to growth of aggregate demand components, first quarter of 2008-second quarter of 2015
(Percentages)

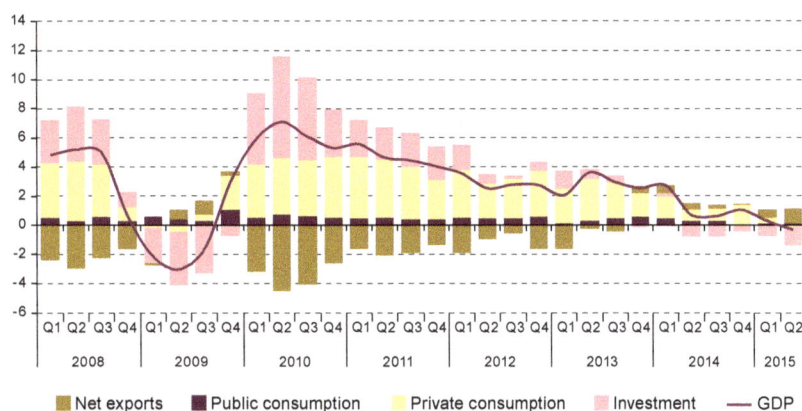

Source: Economic Commission for Latin America and the Caribbean (ECLAC), on the basis of official figures.

Like economic activity overall, the various components of aggregate demand were sharply differentiated by subregion. For example, with respect to 2014 figures, private consumption shrank 1.6% in South America, but rose 4.6% in Central America. Similarly, public consumption almost flatlined in South America, at 0.1%, but climbed 4.4% in Central America.

Gross fixed capital formation was down by 4.2% for Latin America, reflecting a heavy drop (-7.2%) in the South American economies, but was up by 7.0% on 2014 in Central America and by 4.3% for the subregion formed by Central America and Mexico.

A five-quarter run of contraction in gross fixed capital formation beginning in the second quarter of 2014 has brought this variable's GDP share down by 1.5 percentage points, from 21.5% in 2013 to 20.0% in 2015.

Weak domestic demand has been reflected in a 1.1% fall in goods and services imports in real terms, as a result of lower consumption and slack investment in the region overall. Meanwhile, goods and services exports climbed 2.5% in real terms. Given that the region's real imports slowed faster than in 2014, net exports made a slightly larger contribution to growth than last year.

Slowing economic activity is occurring amid negative contribution to growth by industry, with services remaining the strongest contributor

The performance of domestic demand in Latin America was reflected in the decline in economic activity by sector. For simplicity's sake, the different production activities have been grouped in three major sectors. The first, the primary sector, includes agriculture and mining and extractive activities. The secondary sector includes construction, manufacturing and electricity generation, gas and water. The tertiary sector encompasses services activities.

Although all the sectors have slowed, the secondary sector contracted by 1.8% in 2015 on top of a 0.3% decline in 2014. During the same period, the primary and tertiary sectors expanded 1.7% and 0.5%, respectively. As a result, the contribution of the secondary sector to value added growth was negative by 0.43 percentage points, of which the manufacturing sector alone accounted for 0.34 percentage points. The tertiary sector is still the largest contributor, bringing 0.38 percentage points to value added growth, (see figure III.3), while the contribution of the primary sector held steady at 0.12 percentage points in 2015.

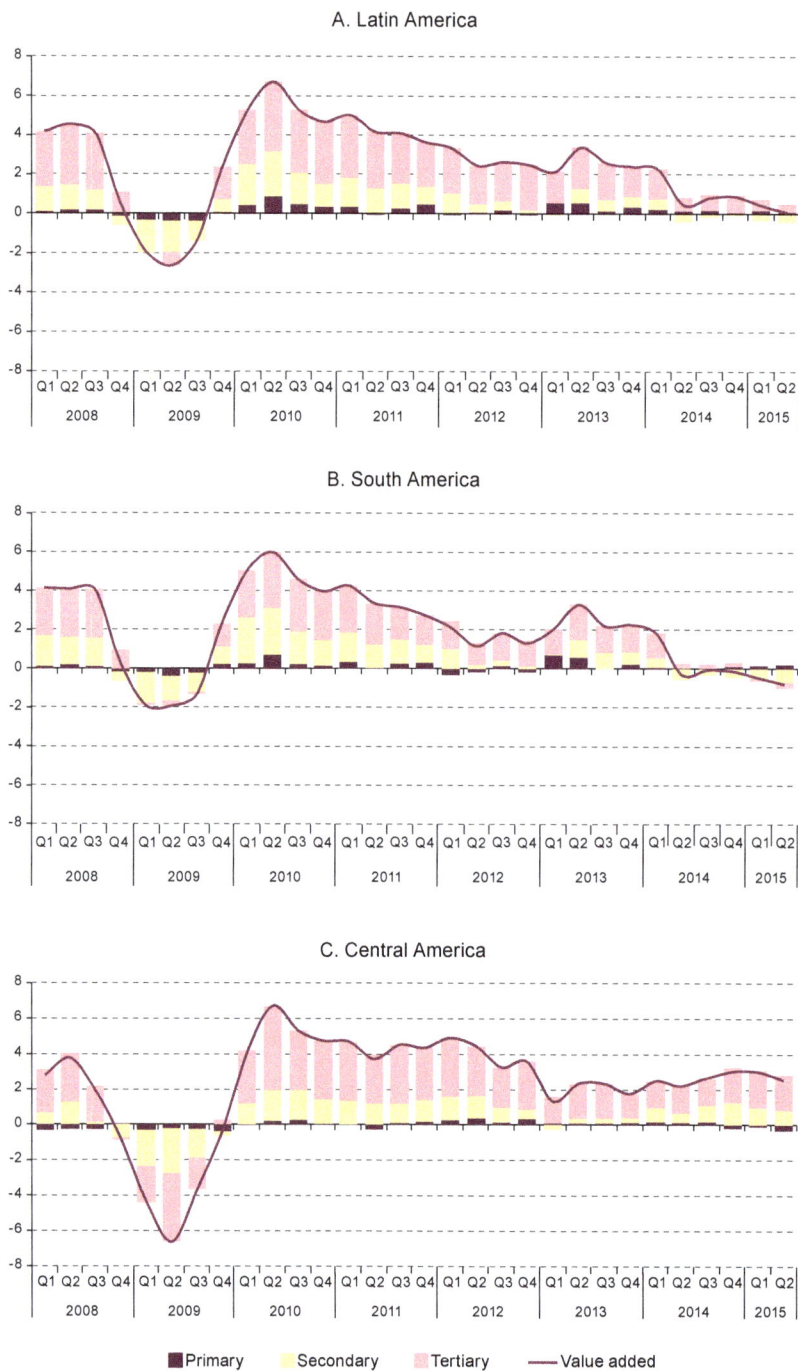

Figure III.3
**Latin America: GDP variation and contribution to growth of the sectors of economic activity,
first quarter of 2008-second quarter of 2015**
(Percentages)

A. Latin America

B. South America

C. Central America

Primary   Secondary   Tertiary   —— Value added

Source: Economic Commission for Latin America and the Caribbean (ECLAC), on the basis of official figures.

Here too, performance is very uneven by subregion. In Central America, the secondary sector expanded 0.6%, but it shrank by 0.3% in South America. Manufacturing performance was worst in South America, where it contracted by 4.2% with respect to 2014.

Amid declining terms of trade, disposable national income grew at below-GDP rates

In 2015, gross disposable national income grew at below-GDP rates for the fourth year running in Latin America.[16] The fall in the region's terms of trade and slow revenue growth in 2015 account for the difference between growth in income and in output.

Again, the variations between subregions were significant. While the South American economies —especially the energy exporters— experienced the heaviest terms-of-trade downturn, the Central American and Caribbean economies benefited the most, as net importers of food and fuels. The region's strongest growth in net income occurred in the Central American economies (14.0%) and Mexico (8.0%), contrasting with the 4.0% expansion posted by the South American economies.

On this basis, gross disposable national income was down by more than a percentage point of GDP, chiefly as a result of terms-of-trade variations and a meagre rise in net current transfers. Conversely, in Central America, terms-of-trade gains and a surge in net current transfers pushed up gross disposable national income by over 5 percentage points of GDP (see figure III.4).

Figure III.4
Latin America: annual variation in GDP and in gross disposable national income, 2003-2015
(Percentages, on the basis of dollars at constant 2010 prices)

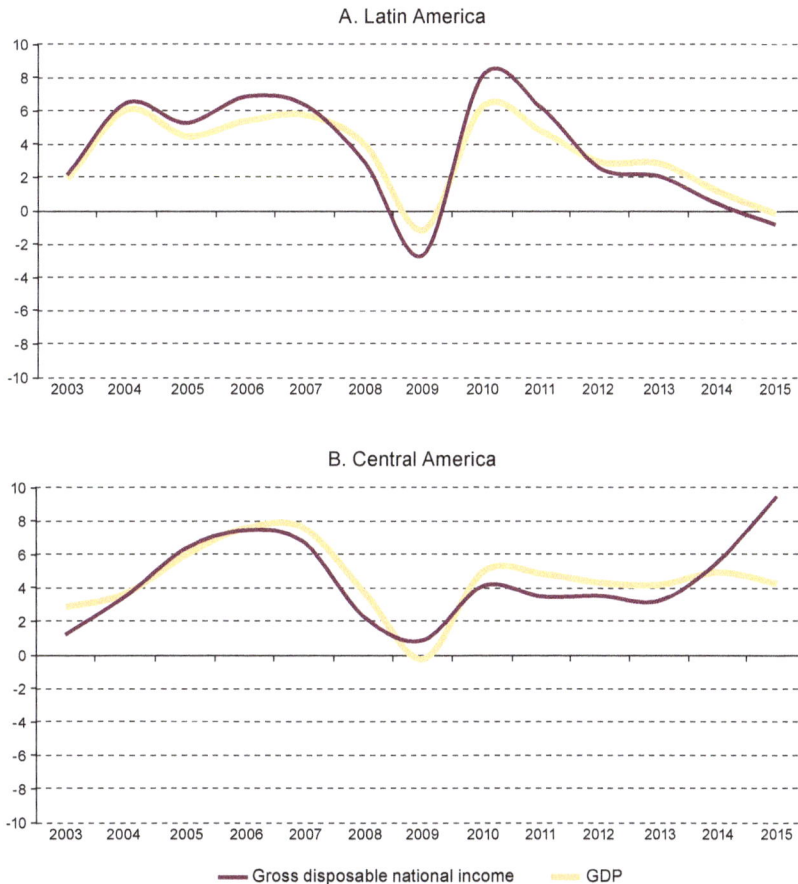

A. Latin America

B. Central America

— Gross disposable national income   — GDP

---

[16] The gap between GDP and gross national disposable income is the result of terms of trade, net current transfers and net payments abroad.

Figure III.4 (concluded)

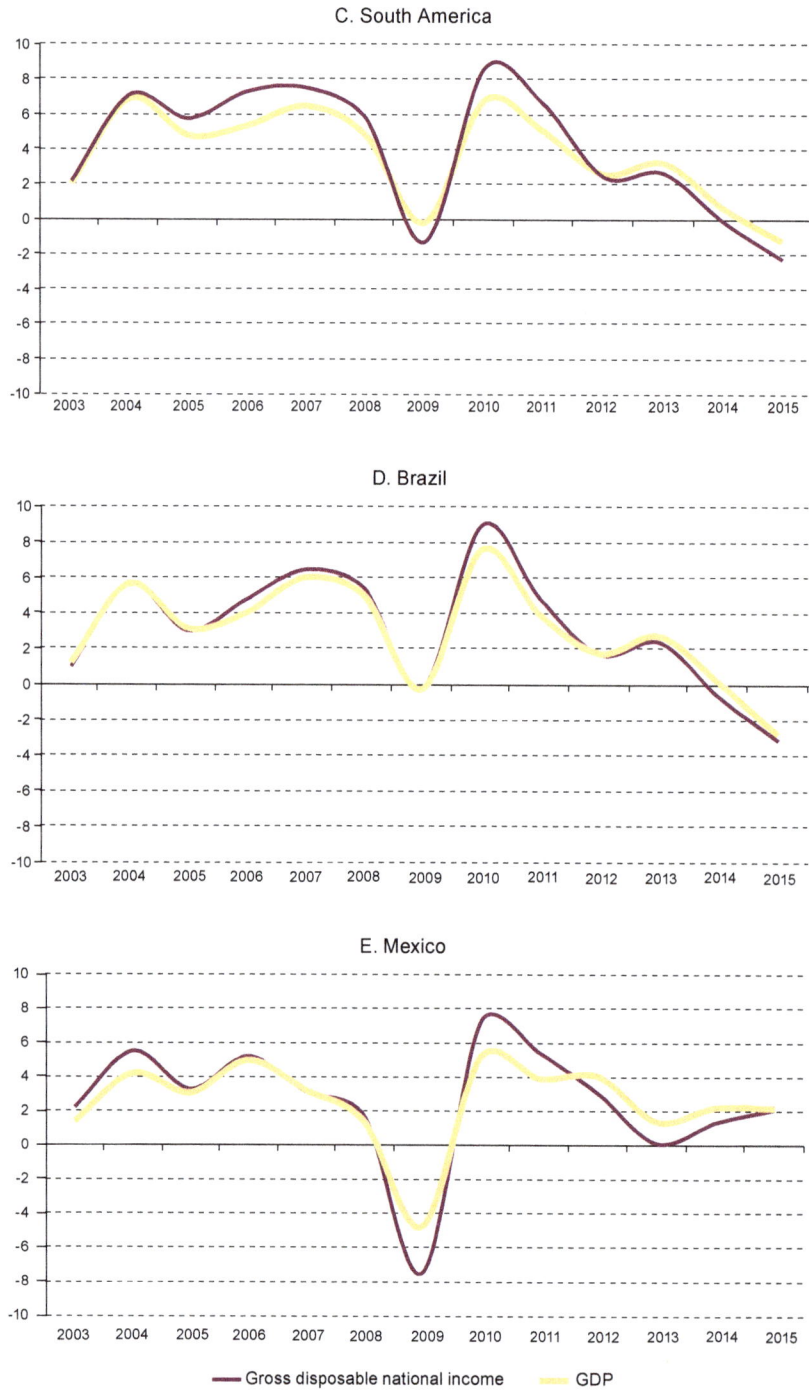

C. South America

D. Brazil

E. Mexico

Gross disposable national income ▬▬ GDP

Source: Economic Commission for Latin America and the Caribbean (ECLAC), on the basis of official figures.

Chapter IV

Domestic prices

Inflation was much the same in 2015 as in 2014 in Latin America and the Caribbean overall, with patterns diverging sharply between the north and south of the region

Inflation in Latin America and the Caribbean as measured by the consumer price index (CPI) was slightly higher in the first 10 months of 2015 than in the same period of 2014, with a cumulative price rise of 6.6% as compared to 6.5% the year before (see figure IV.1).[17]

Figure IV.1
Latin America and the Caribbean (weighted averages): 12-month changes in the consumer price index (CPI), January 2010 to October 2015
(Percentages)

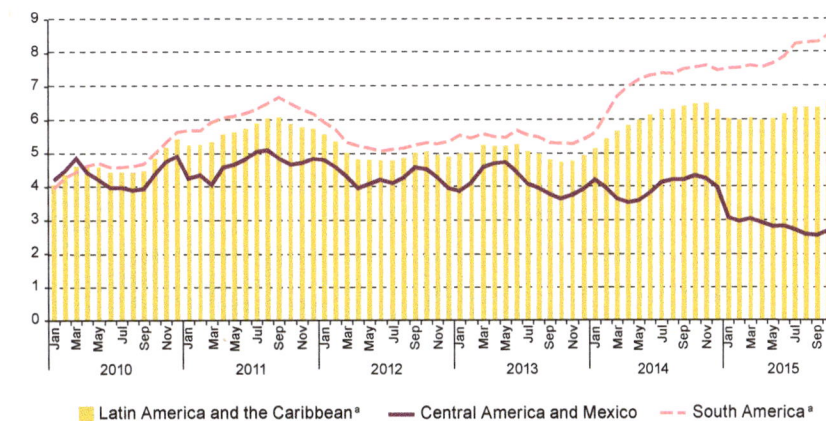

Legend: Latin America and the Caribbean[a] — Central America and Mexico — — South America[a]

Source: Economic Commission for Latin America and the Caribbean (CEPAL), on the basis of official figures.
[a] Excludes the Bolivarian Republic of Venezuela.

The stability of the overall figure notwithstanding, inflation behaved very differently in the first and second halves of 2015. The regional inflation rate was lower in the first five months of the year, at 6.0%, than in late 2014. This was undoubtedly connected to falling prices for commodities, especially energy and food. The situation was reversed in the second half as price rises accelerated, especially in the economies of South America, showing the effects of large depreciations in some of the region's currencies.

---

[17] The regionwide figure is the average of the countries' inflation rates weighted by their share of the region's total population; the Bolivarian Republic of Venezuela has been excluded from the weighting because the country's prices have not been officially published since December 2014.

As noted in the *Economic Survey of Latin America and the Caribbean 2015*,[18] inflation has behaved very differently from one subregion to another. In the economies of the north of the region (Central America, Mexico and the English- and Dutch-speaking Caribbean), the trend of slowing inflation since 2013 became more pronounced in 2015, so that the cumulative change in the CPI for the subregion comprising the economies of Central America and Mexico in the 12 months to October dropped from 4.3% in 2014 to 2.7% in 2015. Indeed, many of the subregion's economies have had negative inflation rates this year, examples being Costa Rica (-0.9%), El Salvador (-2.3%) and Panama (-0.4%). An exception to this trend is Haiti, where inflation accelerated and prices increased by 11.7% from October 2014 to October 2015, which is 5.9 percentage points more than in the 12 months to October 2014.

Inflation also slowed considerably in the economies of the English- and Dutch-speaking Caribbean, with average inflation to October 2015 in this group being estimated at 2.6%, as compared to a figure of 5.6% to October 2014. Once again, the drop in energy and food prices was among the main factors behind this price dynamic in the subregion. In the case of Dominica, a sharp decline in aggregate demand interacted with the factors mentioned to yield negative inflation in 2015.

Inflation has continued to accelerate in the economies of South America, so that the cumulative figure for the 12 months to October rose from 7.6% in 2014 to 8.5% in 2015. At the country level, general inflation was above 9% in Argentina (14.3%), Brazil (9.9%) and Uruguay (9.2%), while in Chile, Colombia and Peru it stayed above the target range set by the monetary authority (see table IV.1). Although no official information is available, it is worth noting that inflation in the Bolivarian Republic of Venezuela has also increased significantly from the 68.5% seen in 2014, with preliminary estimates indicating an inflation rate in triple digits for 2015, as measured by the consumer price index.

Falling energy and food prices on international markets have contributed to the decline in inflation in Central America, while currency depreciation has driven inflation higher in South America

A number of factors lie behind the sharp differences between the economies of the region's north and south, but a key one has undoubtedly been the combined effects of changes in energy and food prices and the dynamic of the region's exchange rates. In the economies of the north (except Mexico and Trinidad and Tobago), the drop in energy prices has resulted in a decline in fuel prices which, given the relative stability of these economies' currencies, has meant lower energy costs and smaller price rises.

Large currency depreciations in the economies of the south of the region, particularly those with more flexible exchange rates (Brazil, Chile, Colombia and Peru), greatly outweighed the effects of falling prices for commodities, including energy, the result being inflation as these exchange-rate shifts worked through to domestic prices.

In the Bolivarian Republic of Venezuela, factors such as a reduced supply of currency for imports (especially in the private sector), an increasing scarcity of both final goods and production inputs, and monetary financing of public-sector operations, combined with an exchange-rate depreciation of over 400% in the parallel foreign-exchange market, caused inflation to rise strongly. In Argentina, meanwhile, the inflation rate eased in 2015, although it remains above 10%.

---

[18] Economic Commission for Latin America and the Caribbean (ECLAC), *Economic Survey of Latin America and the Caribbean: Challenges in Boosting the Investment Cycle to Reinvigorate Growth* (LC/G.2645-P), Santiago, 2015.

Table IV.1

Latin America and the Caribbean: 12-month changes in the consumer price index (CPI), October 2013 to October 2015

(Percentages)

	To October 2013	To December 2013	To October 2014	To December 2014	To October 2015
Latin America and the Caribbean (excluding the Bolivarian Republic of Venezuela)	4.8	4.9	6.5	6.3	6.6
South America (excluding the Bolivarian Republic of Venezuela)	5.3	5.4	7.6	7.5	8.5
Argentina	10.5	10.9	24.2	23.9	14.3
Bolivia (Plurinational State of)	7.5	6.5	3.6	5.2	4.3
Brazil	5.8	5.9	6.6	6.4	9.9
Chile	1.5	3.0	6.1	4.6	4.0
Colombia	1.8	1.9	3.3	3.7	5.9
Ecuador	2.0	2.7	4.0	3.7	3.5
Paraguay	4.4	3.7	3.5	4.2	3.2
Peru	3.0	2.9	3.1	3.2	3.7
Uruguay	8.7	8.5	8.1	8.3	9.2
Venezuela (Bolivarian Republic of)	54.3	56.2	63.9	68.5	...
Central America and Mexico	3.6	3.9	4.3	4.0	2.7
Central America	1.5	1.4	1.5	1.3	1.1
Costa Rica	4.1	3.7	5.7	5.1	-0.9
Cuba	0.2	0.0	1.9	2.1	1.7 [a]
Dominican Republic	4.7	3.9	2.9	1.6	1.2
El Salvador	0.5	0.8	1.9	0.5	-0.2
Guatemala	4.2	4.4	3.6	2.9	2.2
Haiti	4.2	3.4	5.8	6.4	11.7
Honduras	4.6	4.9	6.3	5.8	2.5
Mexico	3.4	4.0	4.3	4.1	2.5
Nicaragua	6.5	5.4	6.8	6.4	2.8
Panama	3.9	3.7	2.1	1.0	-0.4
The Caribbean	4.9	5.2	5.6	4.7	2.6
Antigua and Barbuda	1.3	1.1	1.4	1.3	0.6 [b]
Bahamas	-0.2	0.8	1.5	0.2	2.0 [b]
Barbados	1.8	1.1	2.4	2.3	-0.3 [c]
Belize	0.7	1.6	0.9	-0.2	-0.7 [b]
Dominica	0.5	-0.4	0.7	0.5	-1.7 [b]
Grenada	-1.6	-1.2	0.0	-0.6	-0.9 [b]
Guyana	1.4	0.9	0.3	1.2	-0.2 [b]
Jamaica	10.3	9.7	8.2	6.2	3.5 [d]
Saint Kitts and Nevis	1.3	1.0	0.9	-0.6	-2.7 [b]
Saint Lucia	-3.5	-0.7	5.2	3.7	0.1 [b]
Saint Vincent and the Grenadines	0.8	0.0	0.1	0.1	-1.8 [b]
Suriname	1.2	0.6	4.2	3.9	4.1
Trinidad and Tobago	2.7	5.6	8.9	8.5	4.8 [a]

Source: Economic Commission for Latin America and the Caribbean (ECLAC), on the basis of official figures.
[a] Data to September 2015.
[b] Data to June 2015.
[c] Data to July 2015.
[d] Data to August 2015.

At the regional level, food inflation slowed slightly in 2015 relative to 2014, while core inflation remained unchanged

When the evolution of prices is broken down between core inflation and non-core components (energy and food), it transpires that cumulative food inflation in the region slowed from 7.6% in the 12 months to October 2014 to 7.4% in the 12 months to October 2015, while core inflation, at 6.0%, was similar to that of 2014 (see figure IV.2).

Figure IV.2
Latin America and the Caribbean (weighted averages): cumulative 12-month general, core, food, goods and services inflation, January 2010 to October 2015
(Percentages)

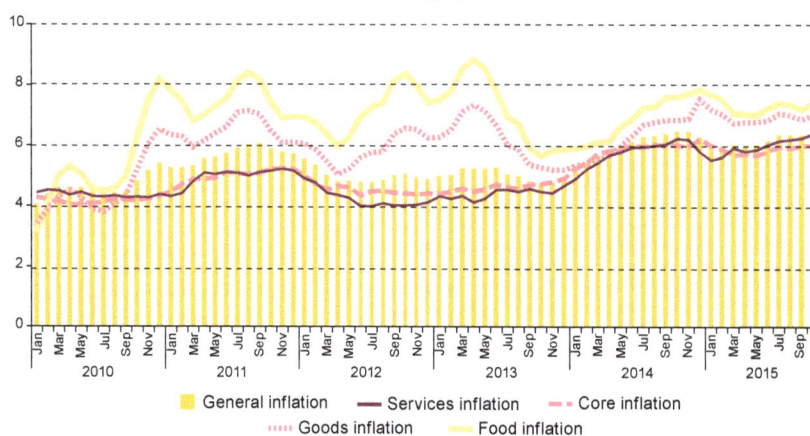

Source: Economic Commission for Latin America and the Caribbean (CEPAL), on the basis of official figures.

At the subregional level, food inflation increased in the economies of South America from 8.1% in October 2014 to 9.0% in October 2015; the rise was 4.4 percentage points in Colombia, but there were declines of 8.8 percentage points in Argentina and 4.7 percentage points in Chile. In the subregion comprising Central America and Mexico, food inflation trended downward from 6.6% in October 2014 to 4.2% in October 2015, and in three economies of the subregion, Costa Rica, El Salvador and Nicaragua, it declined by more than 5 percentage points, while in Haiti it rose by 8.3 percentage points. Food inflation was over 10% in Argentina, Brazil, Haiti, Uruguay and, very probably, the Bolivarian Republic of Venezuela.

Core inflation also picked up in South America and slowed in the Central America and Mexico region, while at the country level it exceeded 10% only in Argentina, the Bolivarian Republic of Venezuela and Haiti. In 2015, taking 12-month price changes to October, the largest declines in the core component of inflation were in Argentina (-9.7 percentage points), Costa Rica (-5.7 percentage points), Jamaica (-7.4 percentage points) and Panama (-6.8 percentage points), while the largest increases in core inflation were in Colombia (3.5 percentage points) and Haiti (6.1 percentage points).

When inflation is broken down between goods and services, the values for both indices in the year to October 2015 were much the same as in the year to October 2014: 7.0% versus 6.9% for goods and 6.4% versus 6.2% for services. In both cases, the regional average reflects, first, higher inflation in South America and, second, lower inflation in the economies of Central America, Mexico and the English- and Dutch-speaking Caribbean.

Different factors will affect the evolution of inflation in 2016

The main factors that might bear down on inflation in future include commodity prices, which are expected to be stable, particularly in the case of food and energy, and the slowing of aggregate domestic demand, especially in the economies of South America.

The main factors that might push inflation up are exchange-rate depreciations ensuing from the volatility on international financial markets, higher external financing costs and the fall-off in foreign direct investment resources, with inflation resulting from the transfer effect of exchange-rate shifts. The effects of climate factors such as El Niño could also drive up prices for agricultural commodities and food.

Which of these factors predominates will depend on circumstances specific to each country, but the presence of one or more of them will certainly shape the actions of policymakers, and particularly those responsible for monetary and exchange-rate management, as they seek to stimulate domestic economic activity, and investment in particular, in a context of slow-growing aggregate external demand. Likewise, changes of policy stance could dramatically alter the trends described above, especially in economies with deep fiscal, exchange-rate and monetary imbalances.

Chapter V

Employment and wages

Whereas an unusually sharp fall in the labour participation rate mitigated the labour market impact of the economic slowdown in 2014, a year later the labour market's adjustment to the cooling regional economy reverted to the more usual historical patterns in Latin America and the Caribbean.[19] In 2015, the decline in labour participation stopped, and the larger number of individuals seeking income in the job market amid slack labour demand pushed up both open unemployment and time-related underemployment. It also caused a deterioration in employment composition, with a larger proportion of employment appearing in low-productivity activities, particularly own-account work, and very sparse creation of wage employment. As a result, average labour productivity declined sharply. In some countries, rising inflation also eroded real wages, which, compounded by the weak growth of employment and its deteriorating composition, reduced household purchasing power.

However, labour market performance varied between the region's countries, with average employment and unemployment rates for the year overall not yet worsening in most cases, whereas the regional weighted average is largely determined by the adverse trend of the labour market in Brazil. Nonetheless, gradual downturn in the labour market became increasingly the rule as the year unfolded.

Unlike the pattern in 2014, the fall in the employment rate has pushed up joblessness, while the composition of employment has deteriorated further

In the second quarter of 2015, the regional participation rate started to climb out of the decline that had begun in early 2013 (see figure V.1); and the urban participation rate is expected to remain at a similar level to the 2014 average for the year overall, in other words 59.8% of the working-age population for the group of 10 countries included in figure V.1.

At the same time, the downturn in the Latin America and Caribbean economy weakened labour demand; and the employment rate, which had started to drop in the second quarter of 2013 from its level in the year-earlier period, fell further, albeit by varying amounts. For the year as a whole, it is estimated to have dropped by 0.4 percentage points.

Consequently, the unemployment rate, which had come down very sharply since 2010 following its spike in 2009, started to climb again in the 10-country group in the first quarter of 2015. Measured as a four-quarter moving average, unemployment reached 6.1% in the second quarter of 2015 and 6.4% in the third (see figure V.2). As an average for the calendar year, a further increase to 6.6% is expected, representing an estimated 1.5 million additional urban unemployed and pushing the total up to 14.7 million.

---

[19] See Economic Commission for Latin America and the Caribbean (ECLAC)/International Labour Organization (ILO)), "Labour productivity and distribution issues", *The Employment Situation in Latin America and the Caribbean,* Santiago, May 2012, which shows how labour market adjustment in a low-growth context occurs mainly through falling employment levels in developed countries, whereas in Latin America and the Caribbean, adjustment occurs mainly through lower average productivity.

Figure V.1

Latin America and the Caribbean (weighted average for 10 countries): [a] urban participation and employment rates, rolling years, first quarter 2011 to third quarter 2015

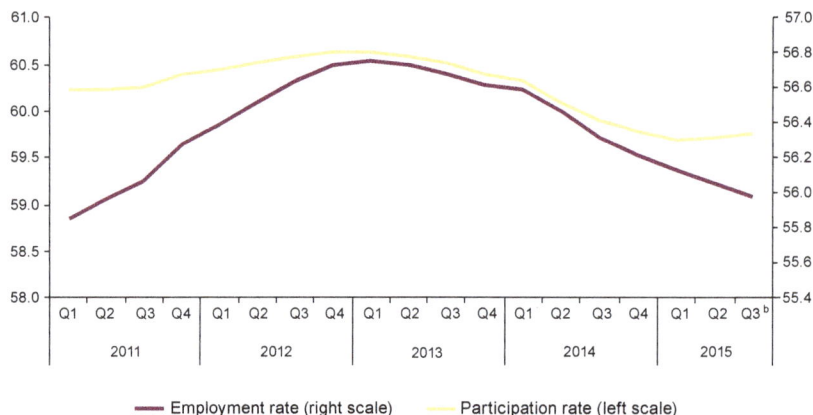

(Percentages)

Employment rate (right scale) — Participation rate (left scale)

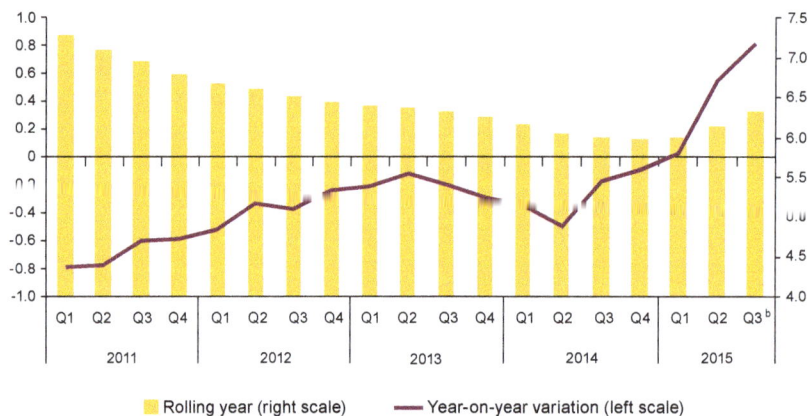

Source: Economic Commission for Latin America and the Caribbean (ECLAC), on the basis of official figures.
[a] The countries included are Argentina, Bolivarian Republic of Venezuela, Brazil, Chile, Colombia, Ecuador, Jamaica, Mexico, Peru and Uruguay. The 2015 figures for the Bolivarian Republic of Venezuela are estimates based on partial data.
[b] Preliminary figures.

Figure V.2

Latin America and the Caribbean (10 countries): [a] urban unemployment rate, rolling year and year-on-year variation, first quarter 2011 to third quarter 2015

(Percentages and percentage points)

Rolling year (right scale) — Year-on-year variation (left scale)

Source: Economic Commission for Latin America and the Caribbean (ECLAC), on the basis of official figures.
[a] The countries included are Argentina, the Bolivarian Republic of Venezuela, Brazil, Chile, Colombia, Ecuador, Jamaica, Mexico, Peru and Uruguay). The 2015 figures for the Bolivarian Republic of Venezuela are estimates based on partial data.
[b] Preliminary figures.

Owing to the weak labour demand, wage-earning employment barely moved in the first half of 2015 (a rise of 0.4%, compared to 0.8% in 2014), measured as the weighted average for the countries with information available, and the total increase in employment (1.3%) represented mainly employment in non-wage categories. In particular, growth in own-account work quickened from 2.2% in 2014 to 2.8% in the first half of 2015, consistently with this category of employment's countercyclical behaviour over the past few years (see figure V.3). In general, but particularly in a context of weak labour demand, this type of work is of worse quality than wage-earning employment; so these contrasting dynamics indicate the deterioration of the average quality of employment.

Figure V.3
Latin America and the Caribbean: economic growth and employment creation, 2000 to the first half of 2015
(Percentages)

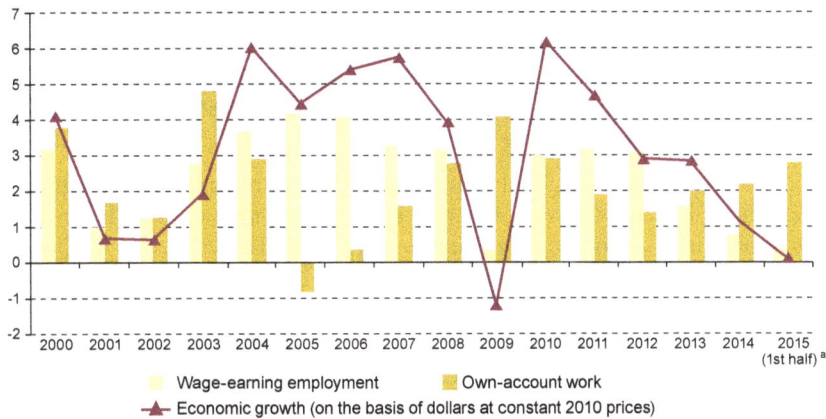

Wage-earning employment Own-account work
Economic growth (on the basis of dollars at constant 2010 prices)

Source: Economic Commission for Latin America and the Caribbean (ECLAC), on the basis of official figures.
[a] Preliminary figures.

Over the past few years, many countries have adopted mechanisms to increase formalization, particularly in wage employment. As a result, in many cases registered employment has outpaced wage employment generally —this was the case in 2015, as well. Nonetheless, in several countries, slackening labour demand is already affecting the growth of registered employment. In Brazil and Uruguay particularly, the number of registered workers shrank in 2015, compared to a year earlier; and in Costa Rica, El Salvador and Peru, it increased more slowly. In contrast, the growth of this type of employment stabilized or accelerated in Argentina, Chile, Mexico and Nicaragua, thanks to the creation of new jobs and the formalization of existing informal ones (see figure V.4).

Figure V.4
Latin America (nine countries): year-on-year variation in registered employment, 2012 to 2015 [a]
(Percentages)

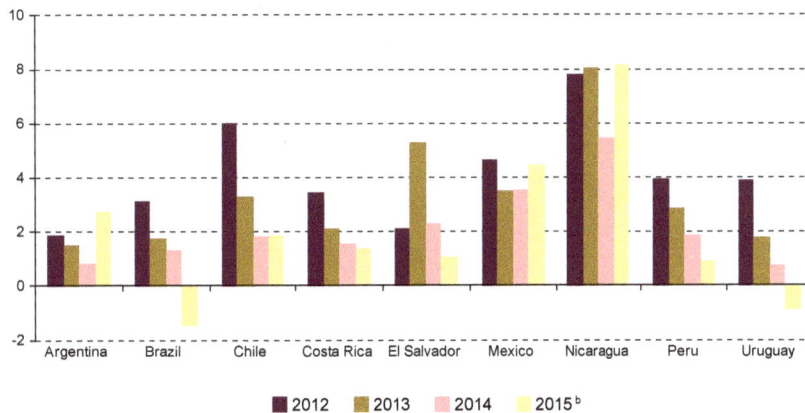

2012 2013 2014 2015 [b]

Source: Economic Commission for Latin America and the Caribbean (ECLAC), on the basis of official figures.
[a] Data refer to wage-earners contributing to social security systems, except in the case of Brazil where they refer to private sector wage-earners reported by firms to the General Registry on Employment and Unemployment Employed and Unemployed, and Peru, where the figures represent employment reported in formal, non-agricultural small, medium and large firms.
[b] The year-on-year variation for 2015 refers to the averages for January-June in the case of Argentina; January-July for Uruguay; January-August for El Salvador and Peru; and January-September for Brazil, Chile, Costa Rica, Mexico and Nicaragua.

Time-related underemployment showed a mixed pattern, although it tended to worsen in more cases than it improved. Nine of the 13 countries with information reported an increase in time-related underemployment, whereas four reported reductions. The overall underemployment figures for these 13 countries have been gradually worsening: while the first-quarter median variation showed a year-on-year fall of 0.2 percentage points, in the second and third quarters the rate increased by 0.1 and 0.4 percentage points, respectively.

In keeping with the general trend of recent decades, most of the new jobs created in 2015 were in the tertiary sector. Nonetheless, compared to the pattern that had prevailed for most of the past decade, when many countries created a large number of new formal jobs in this sector, job growth was moderate in all branches of activity during the first three quarters of the year. In weighted average terms, employment growth in both commerce and services diverged from overall employment growth (roughly 1.3%). Job growth in manufacturing was only slightly slower in the overall figure despite contracting in several countries, owing in particular to the expansion of manufacturing employment in Argentina and Mexico. In many countries, employment in construction reflected the sector's typically procyclical nature and it was up by just 0.7% in the region as a whole. Lastly, agricultural employment sector flatlined.

In the context of a slight shrinkage of regional GDP, a larger volume of employment, led by own-account work, implied a reduction in average labour productivity of roughly 1.7%. This represented a reversion to the region's historical pattern whereby the labour market adjusts to weak economic growth mainly through a fall in labour productivity, unlike what happens in developed countries.

Labour market performance has been uneven, but the indicators show a deteriorating trend overall

As on other occasions, the regional figures are greatly affected by the performance of the region's largest economy; and the sharp deterioration in labour market conditions in Brazil —with urban employment falling by 1.2 percentage points year-on-year and urban unemployment rising 1.9 percentage points on average for the first 10 months of the year— heavily influences the regional weighted averages. This impact has been partly offset by the performance of the region's second largest economy, Mexico, where the urban employment rate rose by 0.5 percentage points, and urban unemployment fell back by 0.8 percentage points in the same period.

Aside from diverging performances of the region's largest economies, the other reporting countries also display widely varying results (see tables A-18 to A-20 in the statistical appendix). Figure V.5 shows that in five of the 14 countries considered, the urban employment rate outpaced the participation rate (countries shown above the diagonal), so open unemployment declined. In four countries, the two rates behaved similarly, and unemployment remained broadly stable; and in another five countries, unemployment rose, in most cases because the employment rate dropped faster than the participation rate.

Figure V.5
Latin America and the Caribbean (14 countries): year-on-year variation in the urban participation and employment rates, 2014 to 2015 (Q1-Q3 average)
(Percentage points)

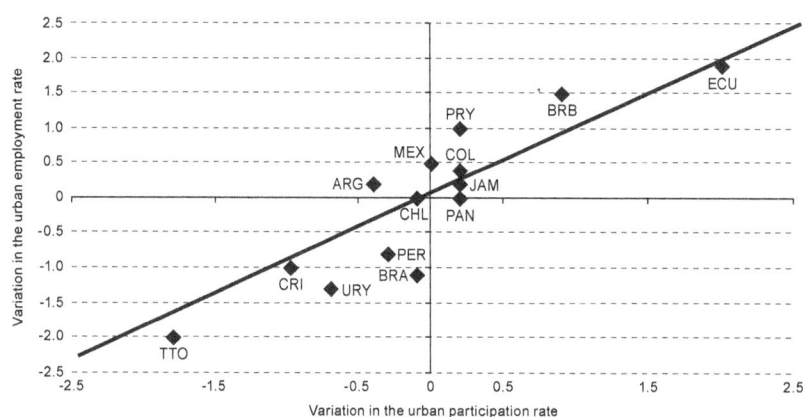

Source: Economic Commission for Latin America and the Caribbean (ECLAC), on the basis of official figures.

Although the worsening of the regional figures is heavily influenced by Brazil and labour market indicators are trending relatively favourably in a number of countries, a deteriorating labour market situation has been the dominant pattern throughout the year. Figure V.6 shows the simple average year-on-year variation in the participation, employment and unemployment rates, with a gender breakdown for countries that have information available.[20]

---

[20] The data shown in figure V.6 differ from those shown in figures V.1 and V.2 not only because they display simple averages rather than weighted averages and report the trend with a gender breakdown, but also because, wherever possible, the coverage included national total data rather than data from urban zones only.

Figure V.6

Latin America and the Caribbean: year-on-year changes in participation, employment and unemployment rates, by sex, first, second and third quarter of 2015 [a]
(Percentage points)

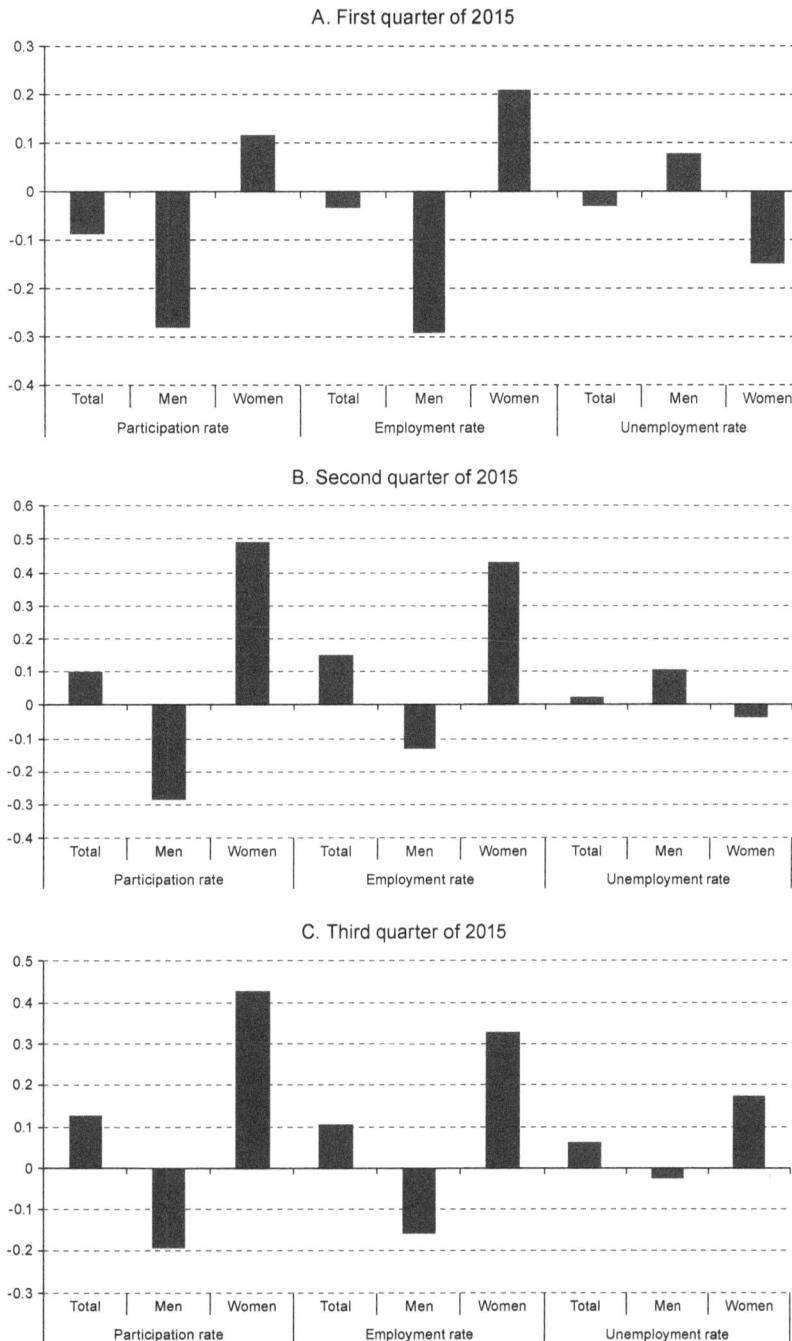

A. First quarter of 2015

B. Second quarter of 2015

C. Third quarter of 2015

Source: Economic Commission for Latin America and the Caribbean (ECLAC), on the basis of official figures.
[a] The countries included for the three quarters are Argentina, Brazil, Chile, Colombia, Costa Rica, Ecuador, Jamaica, Mexico, Paraguay, Peru and Uruguay. Barbados is also included for the first two quarters, and Panama for the first and third quarters.

The figure shows that the previous year's pattern for the region carried over into the first quarter of 2015, with a reduction in the participation rate that far outweighed the fall in employment, thereby allowing unemployment to ease slightly. The situation was more favourable for women, among whom employment growth generated a lower unemployment rate, whereas it rose slightly for men.

Economic Commission for Latin America and the Caribbean (ECLAC)

In the second quarter of the year, both the participation and the employment rates showed an incipient upturn, which halted the slide in the unemployment rate. The results continued to be brighter for women than for men, and the reversal of both rates was due exclusively to women, although the female unemployment rate dropped only slightly year on year.

In the third quarter, the labour market situation showed a clear deterioration, owing to a smaller year-on-year climb in the employment rate, while the rise in the participation rate gathered pace. Consequently, the unemployment rate rose, with the weighted average lagging the urban rate. In that quarter, unemployment increased exclusively for women, whereas in the case of men, the drop in the participation rate prevented a new year-on-year increase in unemployment.

The measurement of unemployment, then, also evidences the labour market situation deterioration over the course of the first three quarters of the year, although not as sharply as in the weighted average, which is heavily affected by the trend in Brazil.

In general, participation and employment rates have both continued to rise among women, while falling slightly for men. As a result, the wide gap between the male and female rates has narrowed somewhat. Although the female unemployment rate did not increase on average in the first half of the year, it rose sharply in the third quarter, suggesting that women are likely to suffer more than men from job shortages amid persistently weak labour demand.

Real wage variation was affected by the differentiated trends in inflation

Real wage trends reflected both the generally deteriorating employment conditions and the heterogeneity that exists between the different countries of the region. Among the few countries with information available on real average wage variations, a slight rise of 1.2% is estimated as an average for 2014-2015, compared to the previous year's increase of nearly 2%. This slower real wage growth reflects smaller average increases in nominal wages, a loss that was not completely offset by the lower inflation among this group of countries. Nonetheless, the situation in Mexico and the Central American countries is very different than that prevailing in South American economies.

In Mexico and Central America, the fall in inflation mitigated the impact of the slower nominal wage growth, so that average real wages grew faster than in 2014. In South America, however, a slight uptick in inflation compounded the gap generated by smaller nominal wages hikes, and real wage growth declined sharply compared to 2014 (see figure V.7).

Figure V.7
Latin America (10 countries): [a] breakdown of the year-on-year variation in real wages by subregion, simple average for 2014 and first three quarters of 2015
(Percentages)

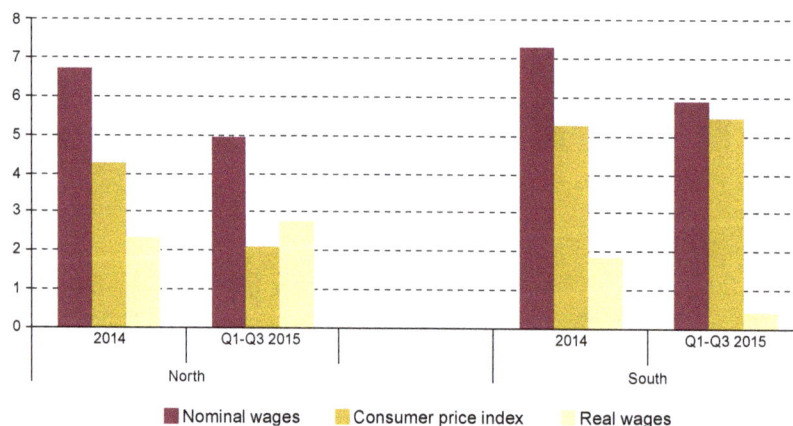

Source: Economic Commission for Latin America and the Caribbean (ECLAC), on the basis of official figures.
[a] The countries included are Costa Rica, Mexico, Nicaragua and Panama for the northern subregion, and Brazil, Chile, Colombia, Paraguay, Peru and Uruguay for the southern subregion.

44

The rise in the average wage was accompanied by higher minimum wages in several countries. In 2015, minimum wage hikes were moderate and the median rise in 18 countries was 2.6%, somewhat less than the previous year's 3.1%. Nonetheless, the minimum wage trend varied across countries. In the Plurinational State of Bolivia and in Panama, minimum wages rose by over 10% in real terms, whereas in Jamaica, Paraguay and Peru, there was no increase in the legal wage, so its value declined in real terms from its year-earlier level.

Although this wage growth, in conjunction with the higher level of employment, has fuelled a moderate increase in household consumption in some countries, private consumption in the region as a whole dipped slightly. Brazil's labour market performance had much to do with this, with the number of employed at a standstill, deteriorating employment composition (a falling proportion of formal wage-earners) and a drop in average real labour incomes, which eroded household purchasing power.

Chapter VI

Macroeconomic policies

A. Fiscal policy

With fiscal strains increasing, the region began to consolidate its public finances

At the central government level, the average fiscal outcome in 2015 is expected to be a primary deficit of 1% of GDP and an overall deficit (including public debt interest payments) of 3% of GDP.[21] For the first time since 2009, all the countries of Latin America are running fiscal deficits, although fiscal revenue and spending levels are considerably higher this year, as figure VI.1 shows.

Figure VI.1
Latin America and the Caribbean: central government fiscal indicators, 2009-2015
(Percentages of GDP)

A. Latin America (19 countries)

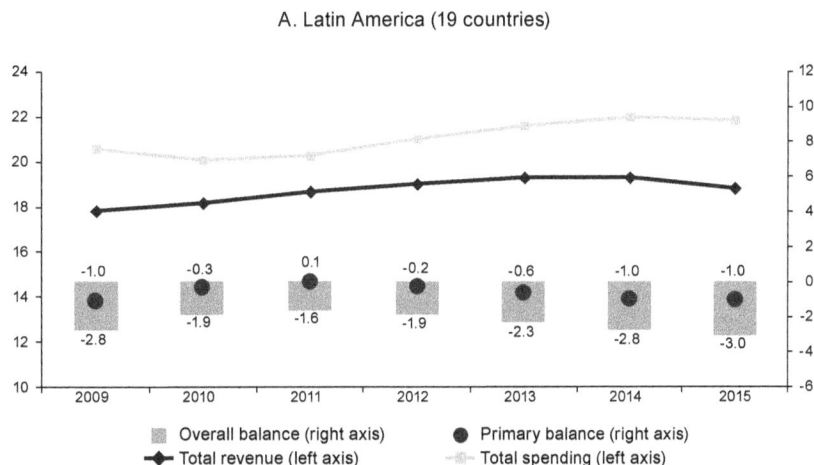

Overall balance (right axis) Primary balance (right axis)
Total revenue (left axis) Total spending (left axis)

---

[21] The figures do not include all government operations, and in some countries the deficit is much larger when public enterprises and subnational governments are included.

Figure VI.1 (concluded)

B. The Caribbean (13 countries)

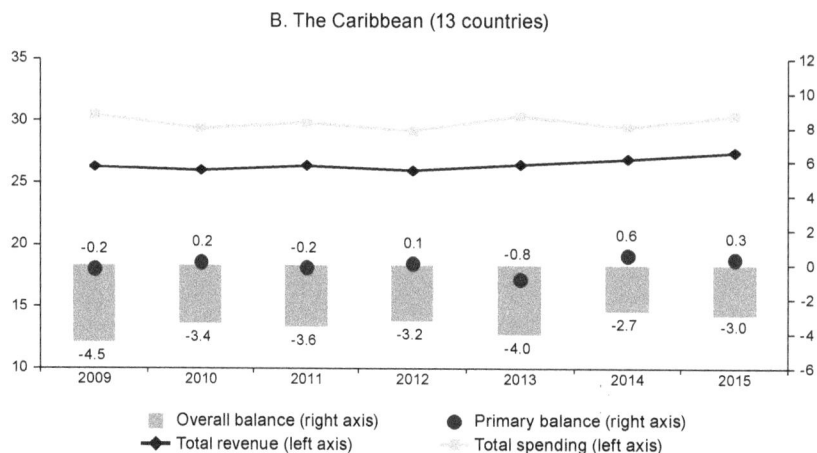

Overall balance (right axis) ● Primary balance (right axis)

◆ Total revenue (left axis) Total spending (left axis)

Source: Economic Commission for Latin America and the Caribbean (CEPAL), on the basis of official figures and budgets and unofficial estimates.

According to the information in each country's official budgets,[22] the fiscal situation in 14 of the 19 countries of Latin America held fairly steady or improved in 2015. In a number of the region's countries, a substantial drop in fiscal revenues resulting from lower export commodity prices was offset by proportional adjustments in public spending.

Fiscal balances improved considerably in Ecuador, El Salvador and Honduras. The fiscal position in Colombia, the Dominican Republic, Guatemala, Mexico, Nicaragua, Panama, Paraguay and Uruguay remained much as in 2014. In Brazil, Chile, Costa Rica, Haiti and Peru, conversely, the fiscal balance worsened substantially (see statistical annex).

In the Caribbean, the average fiscal balance deteriorated, being estimated at -3.0% of GDP for 2015, with the primary balance put at 0.3% of GDP. Eight of the 13 countries in the region improved or saw little change during 2015, with the fiscal balance worsening in just five, among them Barbados, Suriname and Trinidad and Tobago.

The heterogeneity of the macroeconomic performance and productive specialization of the region's countries is reflected in an array of fiscal outcomes. In the Caribbean and Central America, in particular, the public finances have benefited from a significant and positive twofold fiscal shock, with fairly vigorous growth and lower oil outlays.

Most of the countries that have experienced negative external shocks have adjusted their spending levels to keep the public accounts under control and counteract the drop in fiscal revenues, with the budgets presented suggesting the trend will continue in 2016. On average, public debt has held steady as a share of GDP, mainly because interest rates are currently low, although this unprecedented situation could be reversed by future rises.

Latin America's public debt increased slightly to an average of 34.3% of GDP in 2015 (see figure VI.2), still a comparatively low level. However, the rising trend has been explosive in Brazil, where public debt increased by 7 percentage points over the year, this being put down to a worsening fiscal deficit and high government bond interest rates in a context of recession. Public debt also rose in Ecuador (by 3.0 GDP points), Mexico (2.9 points) and Honduras (2.7 points), although to a lesser degree and from a much lower base.

Debt levels are somewhat above average (between 37% and 45% of GDP) in some countries of South America (Argentina, Colombia and Uruguay) and Central America (Costa Rica, El Salvador, Haiti, Honduras and Panama). At the other extreme, debt levels in Chile, Paraguay and Peru are below 20% of GDP.

Debt in the Caribbean countries has generally trended upward over the last half-decade and now averages about 80% of GDP, with Jamaica having the largest public debt at 131% of GDP. Public debt rose during 2015 in Antigua and Barbuda (by 7.9 GDP points), Saint Lucia (3.9 points), Saint Vincent and the Grenadines (3.8 points), Guyana (3.7 points), Trinidad and Tobago (2.8 points), Suriname (2.5 points), Barbados (2.2 points) and Dominica (1.9 points). It dropped in Grenada (by 0.1 points), Belize (1.3 points), Jamaica (2.0 points), Saint Kitts and Nevis (3.5 points) and the Bahamas (3.8 points).

---

[22] The 2015 figures are from revised official budgets.

Figure VI.2
Latin America and the Caribbean: gross public debt, 2015
(Percentages of GDP)

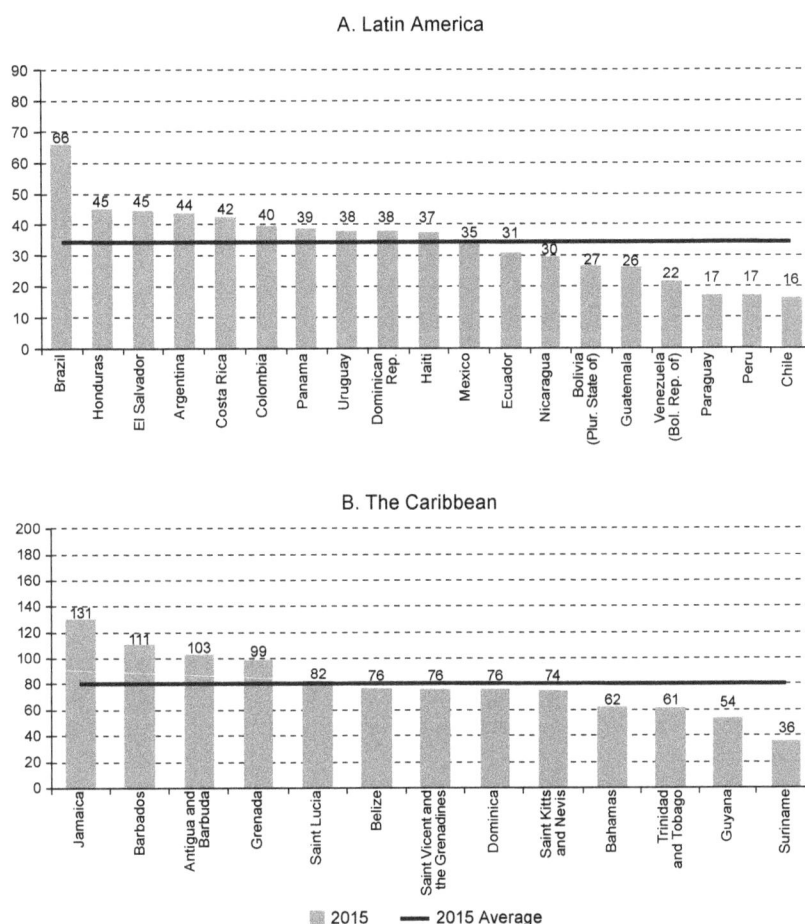

A. Latin America

B. The Caribbean

■ 2015 —— 2015 Average

Source: Economic Commission for Latin America and the Caribbean (CEPAL), on the basis of official figures.

Aggregate public spending, and especially capital spending, declined as a share of GDP

The figures available show certain general trends in public spending. On average, according to the adjustments announced in a number of Latin American countries, capital spending in the region dropped by an average of 0.4 points of GDP, in contrast to the substantial increases of 2014. There were sharp falls in oil-exporting countries (the Bolivarian Republic of Venezuela, Colombia, Ecuador, the Plurinational State of Bolivia and Trinidad and Tobago) and in Brazil, Costa Rica, Honduras, Panama and Paraguay (see figure VI.3). Public investment increased significantly in the rest of Central America and in Chile.

At the same time, although the averages were not much affected, there was a substantial increase in public debt service in several countries. In Brazil, almost the entirety of the rise in public spending in 2015 was accounted for by growth in interest payments (2.7 points of GDP). In other countries (Costa Rica and the Dominican Republic), this expenditure represented a share of over 15%. Debt service has also been growing in Colombia, Ecuador, Honduras and the Plurinational State of Bolivia.

Figure VI.3
Latin America and the Caribbean: disaggregated central government spending, by subregion and country grouping, 2014-2015
(Percentages of GDP)

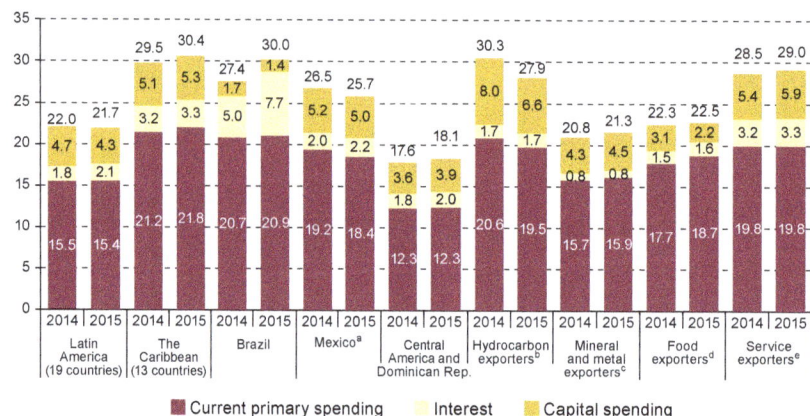

Current primary spending ▪ Interest ▪ Capital spending

Source: Economic Commission for Latin America and the Caribbean (CEPAL), on the basis of official figures and budgets and unofficial estimates.
[a] Federal public sector.
[b] Bolivarian Republic of Venezuela, Colombia, Ecuador, Plurinational State of Bolivia and Trinidad and Tobago.
[c] Chile and Peru.
[d] Argentina, Paraguay and Uruguay.
[e] Antigua and Barbuda, Bahamas, Barbados, Belize, Dominica, Grenada, Jamaica, Panama, Saint Kitts and Nevis, Saint Lucia and Saint Vincent and the Grenadines.

Current primary spending growth moderated on average in Latin America during 2015, after rising continuously as a share of GDP for a number of years. There was a sharp fall in hydrocarbon-exporting countries (1.1 GDP points), contrasting with substantial rises in food-exporting countries (Argentina, Paraguay and Uruguay). In the Caribbean, average current primary spending was up by a substantial 0.6 GDP points, with the largest rises in Bahamas, Barbados, Guyana and Trinidad and Tobago.

Fiscal revenues were affected by lower prices for export commodities, but this decline was partly offset by a rise in tax revenues

Fiscal revenues deteriorated in Latin America in 2015 (see figure VI.4), mainly because of a drop in income from non-renewable natural resources. The collapse of the international crude oil price dealt a blow to the public accounts of the region's producing countries. Overall revenues, and non-tax revenues in particular, declined particularly sharply in Mexico (3.2 GDP points) and the other hydrocarbon-exporting countries (2.6 points). The non-tax revenues of mineral and metal exporters declined yet again (by 0.7 percentage points of GDP in Chile and 0.5 in Peru), in line with the uninterrupted decline in the prices fetched by their commodities that began in 2011. Conversely, fiscal revenues held fairly steady in the Central American countries and increased in the Caribbean.

Although the year was marked by the loss of revenues from non-renewable natural resources, this decline was partly offset in a number of countries by increased tax revenues. On average, Latin America succeeded in increasing tax pressure by 0.2 percentage points of GDP, led by Chile (0.5 GDP points), Mexico (2.2 points) and Ecuador (1.0 points), where recent reforms and measures have generated greater revenues. In Chile, transfers to the tax authorities by the National Copper Corporation (CODELCO) dropped by 22.7% in nominal terms, even as tax revenues increased by 9.3%, driven by a 14% rise in income tax receipts resulting from application of the 2014 tax reform.

In Mexico, oil revenues fell by 2.5 GDP points in 2015, in line with the collapse of the international crude price. However, tax revenues rose substantially (2.2 GDP points), driven by the tax measures adopted in the 2013 fiscal reform. There was a particularly large rise in the income tax take, increasing tax pressure by almost a percentage point of GDP. This was partly due to the application of the new measures, such as abolition of the consolidated taxation regime and improvements to the system for deducting tax from public-sector pay. Another factor behind the improvement in the tax take was reduced fiscal drag from the special excise tax on production and services applied to petrol and diesel (IEPS), which operates as a subsidy whose level depends on international prices for these products.

Figure VI.4
Latin America and the Caribbean: total central government fiscal revenues and tax revenues by subregion and country grouping, 2014-2015 [a]
(Percentages of GDP)

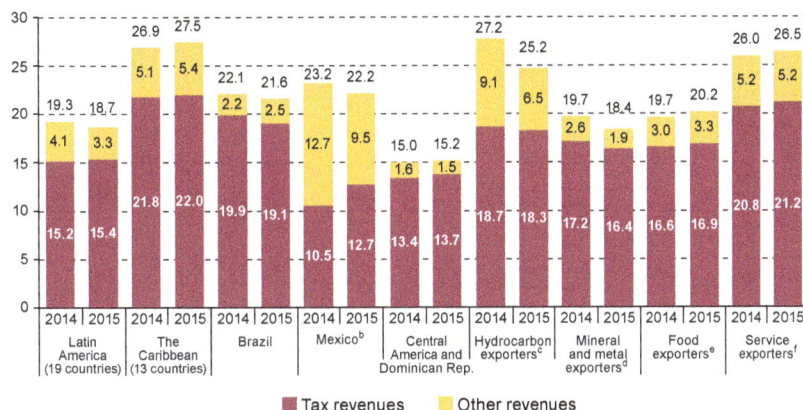

Source: Economic Commission for Latin America and the Caribbean (CEPAL), on the basis of official figures and budgets and unofficial estimates.
[a] The 2015 figures are estimates.
[b] Federal public sector.
[c] Bolivarian Republic of Venezuela, Colombia, Ecuador, Plurinational State of Bolivia and Trinidad and Tobago.
[d] Chile and Peru.
[e] Argentina, Paraguay and Uruguay.
[f] Antigua and Barbuda, Bahamas, Barbados, Belize, Dominica, Grenada, Jamaica, Panama, Saint Kitts and Nevis, Saint Lucia and Saint Vincent and the Grenadines.

Oil revenues in Ecuador also declined greatly over the year, dropping by 1.5 GDP points. Conversely, tax revenues rose strongly (1.0 GDP points), driven by higher receipts from income tax and tariffs. In the case of the former, there was a large temporary effect from the tax amnesty passed in April, which waived up to 100% of interest, fines and surcharges for taxpayers paying off tax arrears. Meanwhile, customs revenues in Ecuador rose by over 50% because of a tariff surcharge applied in March 2015.

In Peru, tax revenues fell substantially (2.0 GDP points) over the year. Fiscal revenues from mining declined anew, mainly because of low corporation tax receipts. This was compounded by a reduction in the rate of this tax from 30% to 28% in December 2014 as part of a package of measures designed to reactivate the country's economy. Revenues from all taxes on income, including personal income tax, payers of which also benefited from a reduction on average, fell by 12% in nominal terms.

Tax revenues in Argentina and Brazil went in opposite directions over the year. In the former, receipts from the profits tax grew strongly (by 45% in nominal terms) to September, as did social security contributions (38%), this being mainly due to the increase in taxable pay. In Brazil, on the other hand, federal government tax revenues dropped by 3.0% in real terms over the first nine months of 2015. There was a particularly large decline in social contributions (3.0% in real terms), in line with the worsening situation in the formal labour market.

In the Central American countries and the Dominican Republic, meanwhile, tax revenues held steady relative to output during the year. However, there was a decline of 0.4 GDP points in Guatemala because of a reduction in receipts from income tax (6.4% in real terms to October) and the value added tax (VAT) on imports (5.7%) that was not offset by the new revenues yielded by measures taken in late 2014, such as a rise in the cement distribution tax, the telephony tax and the vehicle tax.

In the Caribbean, fiscal revenues increased in 2015, reflecting something of an upturn in its economies and the results of fiscal measures taken in recent years. There were particularly large increases in tax revenue in the Bahamas (2.4 GDP points) and Jamaica (1.5 points). In the former, the rise was partly accounted for by implementation of the new VAT. In Jamaica, the growth in tax revenues reflected a large rise in indirect taxes due to VAT changes and an increase in the rates of the selective tax on petroleum products. Meanwhile, Suriname and Trinidad and Tobago saw large drops in revenue from natural resources. Non-tax revenues rose in the latter, however, mainly in the form of capital receipts (up 2.2 GDP points), driven by the sale of Methanol Holdings (Trinidad) Limited and, to a lesser degree, in other countries in the region, by donations associated with natural disasters, such as tropical storm Erika.

B. Monetary, exchange-rate and macroprudential policies

The space available for countercyclical monetary policy may be narrowing, especially in the South American economies

Since the outbreak of the global financial crisis, the region's monetary authorities have geared their efforts towards stimulating aggregate domestic demand, in particular private consumption and investment. Changes in international conditions, including falling prices for primary goods and mounting volatility in international financial markets, together with trends in domestic prices, have eroded the policy space available to central banks and thus curtailed their action.

The South American economies that pursue inflation-targeting policies appear to be running out of space for sustaining expansionary monetary policies, as inflation has gathered pace and begun to exceed the targets set. These economies' central banks thus started raising monetary policy rates in 2015, especially in the second half of the year. In Mexico, the downtrend in inflation has permitted the authorities to leave the monetary policy rate unchanged (see figure VI.5).

Figure VI.5
Latin America (countries with inflation targets): monetary policy rate,
January 2013-November 2015
(Percentages)

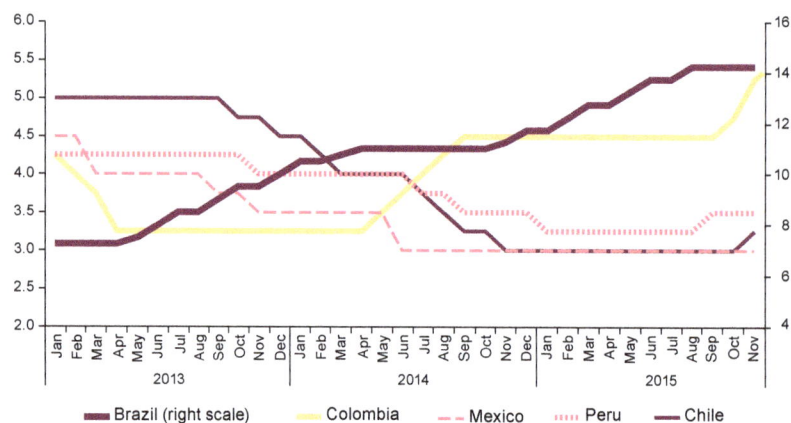

Source: Economic Commission for Latin America and the Caribbean (ECLAC), on the basis of official figures.

In countries whose central banks use monetary aggregates as the main policy instrument, the priority still appears to be to stimulate aggregate domestic demand, since the monetary base is growing faster than in 2014. However, the behaviour of broader aggregates —such as M1 and M2— suggests that despite these efforts, monetary base expansion has slowed in both the dollarized and the English-speaking Caribbean economies and, as of May, in Central America. In the South American economies whose monetary policy is geared chiefly towards monetary aggregates (base money, M1 and M2), growth in these aggregates picked up in the second half of 2014, despite the fact that this group includes some of the region's highest-inflation economies (see figure VI.6).

Figure VI.6

**Latin America and the Caribbean: annualized quarterly variation in M1,
January 2013 to September 2015**

(Percentages)

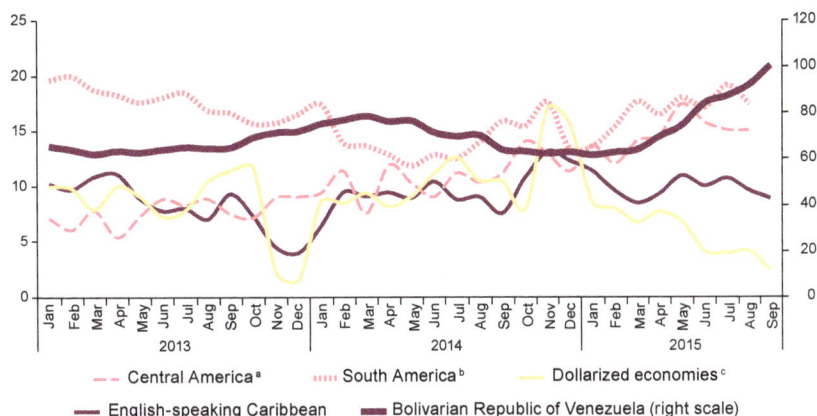

- – – Central America[a]
- ⋯⋯ South America[b]
- —— Dollarized economies[c]
- —— English-speaking Caribbean
- —— Bolivarian Republic of Venezuela (right scale)

Source: Economic Commission for Latin America and the Caribbean (ECLAC), on the basis of official figures.
[a] Costa Rica, Dominican Republic, El Salvador, Guatemala, Haiti, Honduras, Nicaragua and Panama.
[b] Argentina, Paraguay, Plurinational State of Bolivia and Uruguay.
[c] Ecuador, El Salvador and Panama.

Lending rates remained stable amid slowing credit growth

Among the variables sensitive to shifts in policy tools, average lending rates have remained fairly stable, despite the changes in monetary policy instruments.

Credit to the private sector slowed in the dollarized and inflation-targeting economies. In Central America and the English- and Dutch-speaking Caribbean, lending slowed slightly in the first half-year but picked up again in the third quarter. Conversely, in the South American economies whose policy is based on monetary aggregates, lending growth increased in 2015 after slowing in the second half of 2014 (see figure VI.7).

Figure VI.7

**Latin America and the Caribbean: annualized growth in domestic lending to the private sector,
January 2013 to September 2015**

(Percentages)

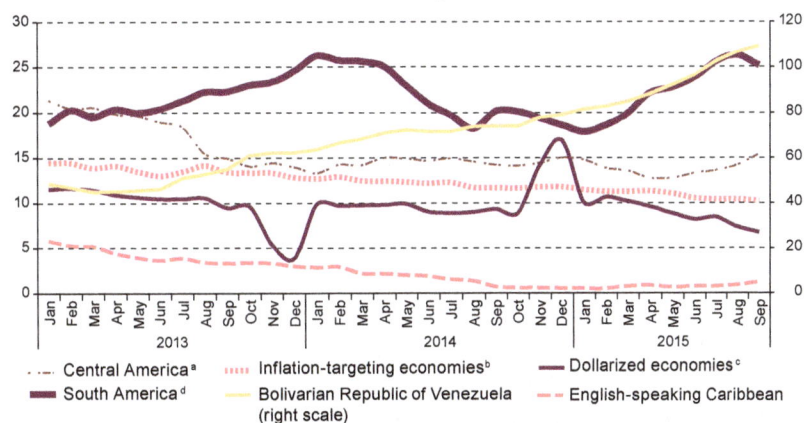

- ⋯⋯ Central America[a]
- ⋯⋯ Inflation-targeting economies[b]
- —— Dollarized economies[c]
- —— South America[d]
- —— Bolivarian Republic of Venezuela (right scale)
- – – English-speaking Caribbean

Source: Economic Commission for Latin America and the Caribbean (ECLAC), on the basis of official figures.
[a] Costa Rica, Dominican Republic, El Salvador, Guatemala, Haiti, Honduras, Nicaragua and Panama.
[b] Brazil, Chile, Colombia, Mexico and Peru.
[c] Ecuador, El Salvador and Panama.
[d] Argentina, Paraguay, Plurinational State of Bolivia and Uruguay.

Analysis of the composition of credit shows a heavy slowdown in lending to industry, whereas consumer lending is the fastest-growing category.

Currencies under flexible exchange-rate regimes depreciated significantly in 2015

Progressively declining international commodity prices and mounting expectations of an interest rate hike by the United States Federal Reserve, together with (to a lesser extent) the gradual slowing of the region's economies, led to a depreciation in the currencies of those countries that maintain flexible exchange rate regimes, in a context of volatility, especially in those economies most integrated with international financial markets. The Brazilian real depreciated by 41% against the United States dollar in the first 11 months of 2015, with respect to the prior-year period, while the Colombian peso depreciated by 36.9%, the Mexican peso by 19.4%, the Chilean peso by 14.6%, and the Peruvian nuevo sol by 12%. These depreciations were even sharper, however, if the reference used is the moment just before the steepest fall in expectations (June 2014), with a loss of 68.9% for the Brazilian real and 58.3% for the Colombian peso (see figure VI.8).

Figure VI.8
**Latin America (selected countries): nominal exchange rate,
January 2013-November 2015**
(Index: January 2008=100)

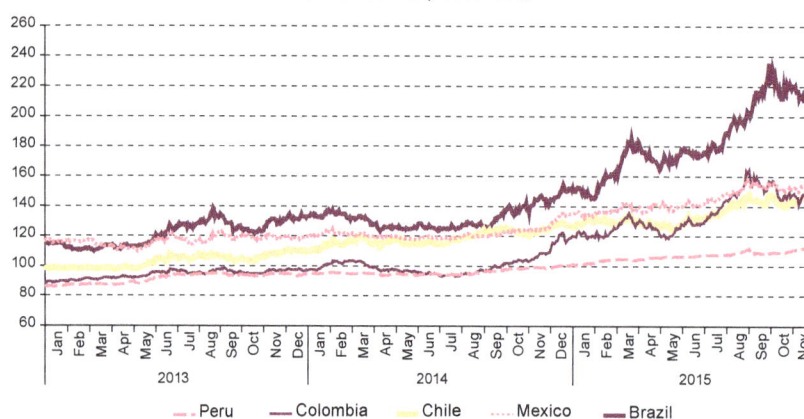

Source: Economic Commission for Latin America and the Caribbean (ECLAC), on the basis of official figures.

The currency depreciations in the countries mentioned were large enough to depress their effective exchange rates, notwithstanding they were often accompanied by rising inflation (associated with pass-through effects, second-order effects, and so forth). Thus, Colombia, Brazil and Mexico experienced year-on-year effective currency depreciation of 25.6%, 23.3% and 12.7%, respectively, in the first 10 months of 2015.[23]

A different situation prevails in countries without flexible exchange-rate regimes. In these cases the real effective exchange rate has been pushed up by combinations of such factors as rising inflation, heavy currency depreciations in these countries' main trading partners and inflexible exchange rates. This has occurred in Argentina, the Bolivarian Republic of Venezuelan, Ecuador and the Plurinational State of Bolivia.

In Central America, Guatemala recorded effective appreciation of 7.4%, as a result of 3.4% nominal revaluation of the quetzal over the first 10 months of 2015 and, to a lesser extent, to depreciation in training partners such as Mexico. In the Caribbean, the process of effective appreciation continued in Trinidad and Tobago, owing chiefly to an almost fixed nominal exchange rate combined with average inflation of 5.5% over the first 10 months of the year, as well as currency depreciation in the economies of main trading partners.

In regional terms, the real effective extraregional exchange rate of Latin America and the Caribbean fell by 0.5% in the first 10 months of 2015, pulled down by effective depreciation of 3.8% for South America. However, the depreciation is much sharper for South America (8.8%) in the comparison between October 2014 and October 2015, and this also had an impact on the figure for the region overall (3.5%) (see figure VI.9).

---

[23] The depreciations are even larger —30%, 39.1% and 17% respectively— if October figures for each year are used for the comparison.

Figure VI.9
Latin America and the Caribbean: real effective extraregional exchange rates,
January 2012–September 2015
(Index: 2005=100)

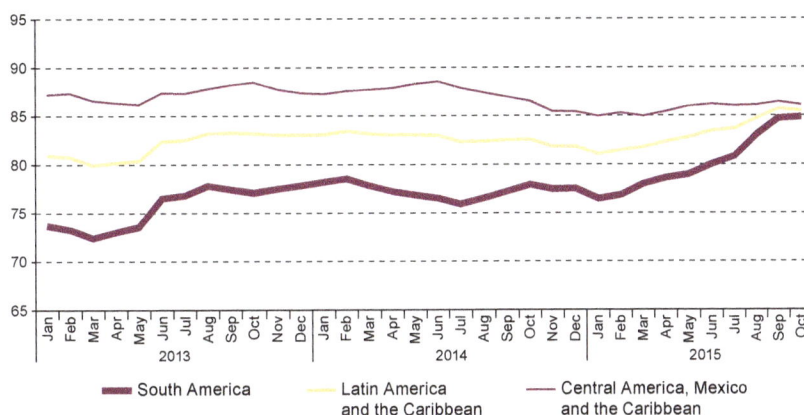

Legend: ■ South America — Latin America and the Caribbean — Central America, Mexico and the Caribbean

Source: Economic Commission for Latin America and the Caribbean (ECLAC), on the basis of official figures.

After a brief upturn in 2014, international reserves declined in 2015

In the first 10 months of 2015 international reserves showed a decline of 3.8% in Latin America and the Caribbean, the largest contraction since the start of the commodity price supercycle that began in 2003. Reserves were down in 22 of the region's economies, and in 13 of these the fall exceeded 5%. The economies with the largest loss of reserves were Argentina (-14.2%), Ecuador (-16.2%), Haiti (-25.1%), Suriname (-36.3%) and the Bolivarian Republic of Venezuela (-31.8%). The level of international reserves in October 2015 were the lowest in Argentina since July 2006, in Haiti since January 2010, in Suriname since November 2007, and in the Bolivarian Republic of Venezuela since February 2003.

Conversely, reserves rose in 10 of the region's economies, with the heftiest gains in Costa Rica (9.7%), Jamaica (17.1%) and Saint Lucia (31.3%). The five economies with the region's largest reserves all experienced reserve losses, with the heaviest falls in Chile (-4.6%) and Mexico (-7.0%).

Figure VI.10
Latin America and the Caribbean: gross international reserves, 2000-2015
(Billions of dollars and percentages of GDP)

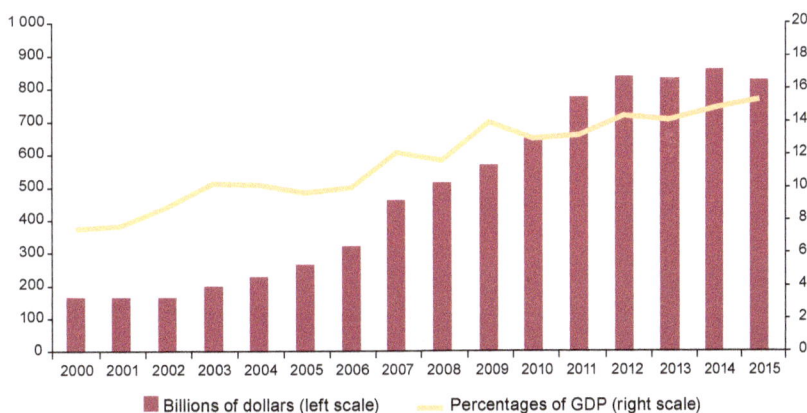

Legend: ■ Billions of dollars (left scale) — Percentages of GDP (right scale)

Source: Economic Commission for Latin America and the Caribbean (ECLAC), on the basis of official figures.

Despite this decline, reserves expanded in relation to GDP, from 14.8% in 2014 to 15.3% en 2015 (see figure VI.10). This performance at the regional level reflected developments in the South American economies (where reserves rose by 7.1%), especially Brazil and Colombia, where the reserves-to-GDP ratio climbed by over 10%, offsetting the fall in the English-speaking Caribbean (-6.3%) and in Central America and Mexico (-4.1%).

The region's countries took macroprudential measures to reduce systemic vulnerabilities

The countries of the region made reforms to their financial systems to complement monetary and exchange-rate policies, adopting macroprudential measures with a view to offsetting potential systemic risks and adapting their international reserves management to increasingly uncertain external conditions and rising foreign borrowing costs.

Changes were made to the regulatory framework in Barbados and Jamaica; to rules relating to corporate bond and derivatives markets in Brazil, Mexico and Peru; to legal reserve requirements on bank deposits in Barbados, the Bolivarian Republic of Venezuela, Brazil, the Dominican Republic, Guatemala and Peru; and to regulations on foreign-exchange allocation in Argentina and the Bolivarian Republic of Venezuela. The dedollarization process was deepened in Peru and the Plurinational State of Bolivia, a new digital currency was proposed in Ecuador, and credit card interest rate ceilings were established in Guatemala.

In addition, new instruments emerged, such as a currency swap agreement between China and several of the region's countries, including Argentina, Chile and Suriname. At the same time, resources from multilateral agencies have shored up the international reserve position in several of the region's economies, including Honduras and Jamaica, and the Bolivarian Republic of Venezuela drew upon funds held with the International Monetary Fund (IMF) and sold gold reserves.

Chapter VII

Risks and outlook for 2016

A number of scenarios and possible risks will arise in the global economy in 2016 and will unquestionably affect the course of economic activity in the Latin American and Caribbean region. As noted earlier, projections for the next few years are for low global growth, sustained by slow but steady recovery in the developed economies. Serious risks remain, however, which could jeopardize that trajectory. Aside from the eurozone's ongoing difficulties, uncertainty has been mounting over the future performance of China and the emerging economies in general. In the case of China, the most likely scenarios point to continued economic slowdown, with a growth rate of around 6.4% in 2016. Trends in the emerging economies are clouding the aggregate external demand outlook for the countries of Latin America and the Caribbean.

To uncertainties over the growth of the global economy is added the lacklustre growth in trade —at 1.5% in 2015, the poorest performance since the crisis of 2007-2009. Global trade volumes are expected to expand at rates of around 2.5% in 2016, still lagging economic growth rates.

Amid slack growth in aggregate global demand and supply-side constraints, raw materials prices are unlikely to recover and will remain at close to end-2015 values. In this context, terms of trade for the Latin American and Caribbean region overall will decline again, although not as steeply as in 2015.

Conditions on the financial markets are expected to toughen with respect to 2015, when emerging economies were already feeling the effects of decreasing availability of financial flows given the uncertainty and volatility that prevailed to a greater or lesser extent for most of the year, along with reduced global liquidity and a gradual rise in the cost of raising funds on the international markets. Accordingly, financial flows to emerging markets, which were down year-on-year in 2015, are unlikely to pick up in 2016. International financial market turbulence is reflecting the effects of possible monetary policy "normalization" in the United States and the strengthening of the dollar.

As in previous years, global economic trends have strongly differentiated effects on the various countries and subregions of Latin America and the Caribbean, and they tend to sharpen subregional differences in terms of the production and trade bias of the economies. Countries that rely on exports of primary goods and have China as a main export destination will be worse affected than those that export manufactures or services to more developed economies, especially the United States.

For primary-goods-exporters, the dip in income from this source will constrain the performance of variables such as disposable national income (and, thus, of private consumption), as well as fiscal revenues (and, thus, of space for countercyclical policymaking), the current account balance and exchange-rate movements. In addition, with inflationary pressure building up owing to exchange-rate pass-through effects, the use of countercyclical monetary policy has been tailing off in those countries.

The combination of tighter liquidity in external financial markets and terms-of-trade shocks will reduce international financial flows to many of the countries in the region, as capital inflows decrease and outflows rise. In turn, this will prolong exchange-rate volatility and oblige the countries to make greater use of international reserves to finance current account deficits, increasing the likelihood that the region is now facing not only an adverse trade environment, but also a much less benign financial environment.

Domestic demand slowed heavily in 2015, as in 2014, especially private consumption and investment, and will likely continue to do so in 2016, which entails significant risks with respect to future growth capacity. In 2015 gross fixed capital formation shrank by 4.2% for Latin America, reflecting a sharp drop in the South American economies (-7.2%). In Central America, gross fixed capital formation was up by 7.0% on 2014, and the figure for the Central American subregion together with Mexico was 4.3%.

Stimulating economic growth poses broad challenges for the region. To achieve this, as well as breaking the contractionary investment cycle begun in 2014, the countries would have to increase productivity, which is also lagging heavily by comparison with other regions and with the developed countries. The capacity to increase productivity has been hampered not only by the drop in investment, but also by the weakening of the region's industrial and manufacturing sectors over the past few years. This weakening has gone hand in hand with increasing deterioration in the labour markets, which are showing rising employment in informal, low-productivity sectors. In a context of slack economic growth, the region must also find ways to safeguard the social progress made over recent years.

Amid declining fiscal revenues, which have set off an entrenchment of the public accounts, it becomes all the more essential to establish fiscal rules to prioritize capital spending. As ECLAC has argued before, it is extremely important to establish countercyclical investment protection regimes in order to stand up to the region's macroeconomic volatility. Regimes that complement countercyclical policies with measures to protect (and stimulate) investment at the bottom of the cycle can be much more effective than fiscal rules based solely on spending or deficit targets when it comes to minimizing adjustment costs and boosting expectations of potential growth and future stability.

Against a complex and risk-prone external backdrop, 2016 is expected to bring slight positive growth of 0.2% (see table VII.1), unlike in 2015 —when the regional economy contracted by 0.4%. Like in 2015, however, the weighted average growth projection hides differentiated performances between countries and subregions. Central America, including the Spanish-speaking Caribbean and Haiti, is projected to grow by around 4.3% in 2016. The inclusion of Mexico, which is expected at grow at 2.6%, brings that average figure up to 3.0%. South America will post negative growth (-0.8%), essentially reflecting contractions in Brazil (-2.0%) and the Bolivarian Republic of Venezuela (-7.0%). Lastly, the English-speaking Caribbean will register growth of 1.6%.

The small upturn projected for the regional economy in 2016 will be too weak to impact noticeably on labour demand and quality employment creation. Although the slightly countercyclical behaviour of labour supply in Latin America overall will prevent the participation rate from rising very much, weak job creation and the resulting fresh drop in the employment rate will again push up the unemployment rate. Low-productivity employment will increase in many countries, since many households will be forced to generate additional labour income.

In several countries, real wages —and thus household income— will be hurt by smaller gains in nominal wages amid rising unemployment, or by relatively high inflation as a lagged consequence of exchange-rate depreciation, for example. This will not occur across the board, however, and real wages should continue to perform more favourably in countries with low inflation and moderate GDP growth.

Table VII.1

Latin America and the Caribbean: annual growth in gross domestic product, 2010-2016

(Percentages, on the basis of dollars at constant 2010 prices)

Country	2010	2011	2012	2013	2014	2015[a]	2016[b]
Argentina	9.5	8.4	0.8	2.9	0.5	2.0	0.8
Bolivia (Plurinational State of)	4.1	5.2	5.1	6.8	5.5	4.5	4.5
Brazil	7.6	3.9	1.8	2.7	0.1	-3.5	-2.0
Chile	5.8	5.8	5.5	4.2	1.9	2.0	2.1
Colombia	4.0	6.6	4.0	4.9	4.6	3.1	3.0
Costa Rica	5.0	4.5	5.2	3.4	3.5	2.7	3.3
Cuba	2.4	2.8	3.0	2.7	1.3	4.0	4.2
Dominican Republic	8.3	2.8	2.6	4.8	7.3	6.6	5.2
Ecuador	3.5	7.9	5.6	4.6	3.7	0.4	0.3
El Salvador	1.4	2.2	1.9	1.8	2.0	2.4	2.4
Guatemala	2.9	4.2	3.0	3.7	4.2	3.9	4.0
Haiti	-5.5	5.5	2.9	4.3	2.7	2.0	2.5
Honduras	3.7	3.8	4.1	2.8	3.1	3.4	3.3
Mexico	5.2	3.9	4.0	1.4	2.2	2.5	2.6
Nicaragua	3.2	6.2	5.1	4.5	4.7	4.0	4.3
Panama	5.8	11.8	9.2	6.6	6.1	5.9	6.2
Paraguay	13.1	4.3	-1.2	14.0	4.7	2.9	3.0
Peru	8.3	6.3	6.1	5.9	2.4	2.8	3.4
Uruguay	7.8	5.2	3.3	5.1	3.5	1.5	1.5
Venezuela (Bolivarian Republic of)	-1.5	4.2	5.6	1.3	-4.0	-7.1	-7.0
Subtotal for Latin America [a]	6.3	4.7	2.9	2.9	1.2	-0.4	0.2
Antigua and Barbuda	-7.1	-1.8	4.0	-0.3	4.8	3.2	3.8
Bahamas	1.5	0.6	2.2	0.0	1.0	1.5	2.4
Barbados	0.3	0.8	0.3	-0.1	0.2	0.5	1.0
Belize	3.3	2.1	3.8	1.5	3.4	1.7	2.7
Dominica	0.7	-0.1	-1.3	0.6	4.0	-2.7	5.2
Grenada	-0.5	0.8	-1.2	2.4	5.7	3.4	2.4
Guyana	4.4	5.4	4.8	5.2	3.8	2.0	3.4
Jamaica	-1.5	1.7	-0.6	0.5	0.7	1.0	1.5
Saint Kitts and Nevis	-3.2	1.7	-1.2	5.8	6.9	5.2	4.7
Saint Lucia	-1.7	0.7	-1.1	0.1	0.5	1.3	1.0
Saint Vincent and the Grenadines	-3.4	-0.4	1.4	1.7	0.7	1.0	2.1
Suriname	5.2	5.3	3.1	2.9	3.4	2.2	2.4
Trinidad and Tobago	3.3	-0.3	1.3	2.3	-1.0	0.2	0.6
Subtotal for the Caribbean	1.4	1.0	1.2	1.5	0.7	1.0	1.6
Latin America and the Caribbean	6.2	4.7	2.9	2.8	1.2	-0.4	0.2
Central America (9 countries) [c]	4.1	4.4	4.0	3.8	4.0	4.4	4.3
South America (10 countries) [d]	6.7	5.0	2.6	3.2	0.6	-1.6	-0.8

Source: Economic Commission for Latin America and the Caribbean (ECLAC), on the basis of official figures.
[a] Estimates.
[b] Projections.
[c] Includes Costa Rica, Cuba, Dominican Republic, El Salvador, Guatemala, Haiti, Honduras, Nicaragua and Panama.
[d] Includes Argentina, Bolivarian Republic of Venezuela, Brazil, Chile, Colombia, Ecuador, Paraguay, Peru, Plurinational State of Bolivia and Uruguay.

Statistical annex

Table A.1
Latin America and the Caribbean: main economic indicators

	2006	2007	2008	2009	2010	2011	2012	2013	2014	2015 [a]
					Annual growth rates					
Gross domestic product [b]	5.4	5.8	3.9	-1.2	6.2	4.7	2.9	2.8	1.2	-0.4
Per capita gross domestic product [b]	4.0	4.4	2.6	-2.4	4.9	3.5	1.7	1.7	0.0	-1.5
Consumer prices [c]	4.4	5.6	7.0	3.5	5.4	5.7	4.9	4.9	6.3	6.6
					Percentages					
Urban open unemployment	8.6	7.9	7.3	8.1	7.3	6.7	6.4	6.2	6.0	6.6
Total gross external debt / GDP [d][e]	36.1	31.7	28.9	29.7	27.5	26.4	28.0	29.6	31.7	33.0
Total gross external debt / exports of goods and services	83.7	82.3	75.3	102.6	98.0	89.3	95.9	101.2	113.4	134.9
Balance of payments [e]					Millions of dollars					
Current account balance	16 866	-10 314	-74 299	-29 899	-103 050	-128 575	-134 144	-158 631	-182 898	-166 858
Exports of goods f.o.b.	609 398	691 818	783 586	630 563	807 317	989 125	1 001 556	1 006 496	990 781	875 990
Imports of goods f.o.b.	543 266	641 993	786 611	590 517	784 539	962 889	993 397	1 027 869	1 027 322	931 447
Services trade balance	-16 779	-20 733	-25 748	-28 360	-42 587	-55 054	-56 670	-61 304	-63 551	-50 301
Income balance	-93 913	-103 538	-110 733	-97 300	-143 101	-161 224	-146 012	-136 790	-145 750	-125 878
Net current transfers	61 426	64 133	65 206	55 715	59 861	61 467	60 378	60 836	62 943	64 778
Capital and financial balance [f]	40 888	139 050	100 165	87 563	196 784	237 834	194 286	178 542	220 013	138 819
Net foreign direct investment	33 661	89 139	96 575	72 412	109 359	137 300	144 998	141 078	137 251	...
Other capital movements	7 226	49 911	3 590	15 151	87 425	100 534	49 288	37 464	82 762	...
Overall balance	57 754	128 736	25 866	57 664	93 734	109 258	60 142	19 911	37 115	-28 038
Variation in reserve assets [g]	-45 246	-130 961	-29 892	-61 384	-94 318	-109 563	-60 198	-20 183	-36 293	28 028
Other financing	-12 508	2 225	4 026	3 720	584	305	56	272	-822	11
Net transfer of resources	-65 533	37 736	-6 541	-6 017	54 267	76 914	48 330	42 023	73 442	13 902
International reserves	319 340	459 581	512 727	567 444	655 389	773 631	835 735	830 009	857 437	824 795
Fiscal sector [h]					Percentages of GDP					
Overall balance	0.1	0.3	-0.4	-2.8	-1.9	-1.6	-1.9	-2.3	-2.8	-3.0
Primary balance	2.3	2.2	1.2	-1.0	-0.3	0.1	-0.2	-0.6	-1.0	-1.0
Total revenue	18.5	18.9	19.0	17.8	18.2	18.6	18.9	19.2	19.3	18.7
Tax revenue	13.9	14.3	14.2	13.6	13.8	14.4	14.8	14.9	15.2	15.3
Total expenditure	18.4	18.6	19.4	20.6	20.1	20.2	20.9	21.5	22.0	21.7
Capital expenditure	3.3	3.7	4.0	4.2	4.2	4.2	4.5	4.7	4.7	4.3
Central-government public debt	35.2	30.3	28.7	30.6	29.2	29.1	30.7	32.2	33.2	34.3
Public debt of the non-financial public-sector	37.4	32.3	30.8	32.8	31.8	31.4	32.9	34.5	35.9	37.0

Source: Economic Commission for Latin America and the Caribbean (ECLAC), on the basis of official figures.
[a] Preliminary figures.
[b] Based on official figures expressed in 2010 dollars.
[c] December - December variation. Weighted average, does not include the Bolivarian Republic of Venezuela.
[d] Estimates based on figures denominated in dollars at current prices.
[e] Does not include the Caribbean, Cuba and the Bolivarian Republic of Venezuela.
[f] Includes errors and omissions.
[g] A minus sign (-) indicates an increase in reserve assets.
[h] Coverage corresponds to the central government. Simple averages for 19 countries.

Table A.2
Latin America and the Caribbean: gross domestic product
(Annual growth rates)

	2006	2007	2008	2009	2010	2011	2012	2013	2014	2015 [a]
Latin America and the Caribbean [b]	5.4	5.8	3.9	-1.2	6.2	4.7	2.9	2.8	1.2	-0.4
Latin America	5.4	5.7	4.0	-1.2	6.3	4.7	2.9	2.9	1.2	-0.4
Argentina	8.4	8.0	3.1	0.1	9.5	8.4	0.8	2.9	0.5	2.0
Bolivia (Plurinational State of)	4.8	4.6	6.1	3.4	4.1	5.2	5.1	6.8	5.5	4.5
Brazil	4.0	6.0	5.0	-0.2	7.6	3.9	1.8	2.7	0.1	-3.5
Chile	4.6	4.6	3.7	-1.0	5.8	5.8	5.5	4.2	1.9	2.0
Colombia	6.7	6.9	3.5	1.7	4.0	6.6	4.0	4.9	4.6	3.1
Costa Rica	8.8	7.9	2.7	-1.0	5.0	4.5	5.2	3.4	3.5	2.7
Cuba	12.1	7.3	4.1	1.5	2.4	2.8	3.0	2.7	1.3	4.0
Dominican Republic	10.7	8.5	3.1	0.9	8.3	2.8	2.6	4.8	7.3	6.6
Ecuador	4.4	2.2	6.4	0.6	3.5	7.9	5.6	4.6	3.7	0.4
El Salvador	3.9	3.8	1.3	-3.1	1.4	2.2	1.9	1.8	2.0	2.4
Guatemala	5.4	6.3	3.3	0.5	2.9	4.2	3.0	3.7	4.2	3.9
Haiti	2.3	3.3	0.8	3.1	-5.5	5.5	2.9	4.3	2.7	2.0
Honduras	6.6	6.2	4.2	-2.4	3.7	3.8	4.1	2.8	3.1	3.4
Mexico	5.0	3.2	1.4	-4.7	5.2	3.9	4.0	1.4	2.2	2.5
Nicaragua	4.2	5.3	2.9	-2.8	3.2	6.2	5.1	4.5	4.7	4.0
Panama	8.5	12.1	8.6	1.6	5.8	11.8	9.2	6.6	6.1	5.9
Paraguay	4.8	5.4	6.4	-4.0	13.1	4.3	-1.2	14.0	4.7	2.9
Peru	7.5	8.5	9.1	1.1	8.3	6.3	6.1	5.9	2.4	2.8
Uruguay	4.1	6.5	7.2	4.2	7.8	5.2	3.3	5.1	3.5	1.5
Venezuela (Bolivarian Republic of)	9.9	8.8	5.3	-3.2	-1.5	4.2	5.6	1.3	-4.0	-7.1
The Caribbean	8.0	6.5	1.4	-3.4	1.4	1.0	1.2	1.5	0.6	1.0
Antigua and Barbuda	13.4	9.5	0.1	-12.0	-7.1	-1.8	4.0	-0.3	4.8	3.2
Bahamas	2.5	1.4	-2.3	-4.2	1.5	0.6	2.2	0.0	1.0	1.5
Barbados	5.7	1.7	0.3	-1.5	0.3	0.8	0.3	-0.1	0.2	0.5
Belize	4.6	1.1	3.2	0.7	3.3	2.1	3.8	1.5	3.4	1.7
Dominica	4.7	6.4	7.1	-1.2	0.7	-0.1	-1.3	0.6	4.0	-2.7
Grenada	-4.0	6.1	0.9	-6.6	-0.5	0.8	-1.2	2.4	5.7	3.4
Guyana	5.1	7.0	2.0	3.3	4.4	5.4	4.8	5.2	3.8	2.0
Jamaica	2.9	17.1	-0.7	-4.4	-1.5	1.7	-0.6	0.5	0.7	1.0
Saint Kitts and Nevis	5.9	2.8	4.1	-5.6	-3.2	1.7	-1.2	5.8	6.9	5.2
Saint Lucia	8.2	0.6	2.8	-0.5	-1.7	0.7	-1.1	0.1	0.5	1.3
Saint Vincent and the Grenadines	7.7	-1.6	6.7	-2.1	-3.4	-0.4	1.4	1.7	0.7	1.0
Suriname	11.4	5.1	4.1	3.0	5.2	5.3	3.1	2.9	1.8	2.2
Trinidad and Tobago	14.4	4.5	3.4	-4.4	3.3	-0.3	1.3	2.3	-1.0	0.2

Source: Economic Commission for Latin America and the Caribbean (ECLAC), on the basis of official figures.
[a] Preliminary figures.
[b] Based on official figures expressed in dollars at constant 2010 prices.

Table A.3
Latin America and the Caribbean: per capita gross domestic product
(Annual growth rates)

	2006	2007	2008	2009	2010	2011	2012	2013	2014	2015 [a]
América Latina y el Caribe [b]	4.0	4.4	2.6	-2.4	4.9	3.5	1.7	1.7	0.0	-1.5
América Latina	4.0	4.4	2.6	-2.4	5.0	3.5	1.7	1.7	0.0	-1.5
Argentina	7.2	6.8	2.0	-1.0	8.3	7.3	-0.2	1.8	-0.6	1.0
Bolivia (Plurinational State of)	3.0	2.8	4.3	1.6	2.4	3.5	3.4	5.1	3.8	2.9
Brazil	2.7	4.8	3.8	-1.3	6.4	2.9	0.8	1.8	-0.8	-4.3
Chile	3.4	3.4	2.5	-2.1	4.6	4.7	4.3	3.1	0.8	0.9
Colombia	5.4	5.6	2.3	0.5	2.8	5.5	3.0	3.9	3.6	2.2
Costa Rica	7.3	6.5	1.3	-2.3	3.6	3.2	3.9	2.3	2.4	1.6
Cuba	11.9	7.2	4.1	1.4	2.3	2.7	2.8	2.6	1.1	3.9
Dominican Republic	9.1	7.0	1.7	-0.4	6.9	1.5	1.3	3.5	6.1	5.4
Ecuador	2.7	0.5	4.6	-1.1	1.8	6.2	4.0	2.9	2.1	-1.1
El Salvador	3.5	3.4	0.9	-3.5	1.0	1.8	1.5	1.4	1.5	2.0
Guatemala	3.0	3.9	1.0	-1.6	0.7	2.0	0.8	1.6	2.1	1.9
Haiti	0.6	1.7	-0.7	1.5	-6.9	4.0	1.4	2.9	1.3	0.7
Honduras	4.6	4.3	2.4	-4.1	2.1	2.2	2.6	1.3	1.6	2.0
Mexico	3.4	1.6	-0.3	-6.3	3.6	2.4	2.6	0.0	0.9	1.2
Nicaragua	2.8	3.9	1.5	-4.0	1.9	4.9	3.9	3.3	3.5	2.8
Panama	6.6	10.2	6.7	-0.1	4.0	9.9	7.4	4.9	4.4	4.2
Paraguay	3.2	4.0	4.9	-5.2	11.6	2.9	-2.6	12.5	3.3	1.6
Peru	6.2	7.2	7.8	-0.1	7.0	4.9	4.7	4.5	1.0	1.5
Uruguay	3.9	6.3	6.8	3.9	7.5	4.8	3.0	4.7	3.1	1.1
Venezuela (Bolivarian Republic of)	8.1	7.0	3.6	-4.7	-2.9	2.7	4.2	-0.0	-5.3	-8.3
The Caribbean	7.2	5.8	0.7	-4.0	0.7	0.4	0.6	0.9	0.0	0.4
Antigua and Barbuda	12.2	8.3	-1.0	-13.0	-8.1	-2.8	2.9	-1.4	3.8	2.2
Bahamas	0.5	-0.5	-4.1	-5.8	-0.2	-1.0	0.7	-1.4	-0.4	0.2
Barbados	5.3	1.3	-0.1	-1.9	-0.1	0.4	-0.0	-0.4	-0.1	0.2
Belize	1.9	-1.5	0.6	-1.8	0.9	-0.2	1.5	-0.7	1.2	-0.4
Dominica	4.4	6.2	7.0	-1.3	0.4	-0.4	-1.6	0.1	3.5	-3.2
Grenada	-4.3	5.8	0.6	-6.9	-0.9	0.4	-1.5	1.9	5.2	2.9
Guyana	5.0	6.7	1.6	3.0	4.0	5.1	4.5	4.9	3.5	1.6
Jamaica	2.4	16.6	-1.2	-4.9	-1.9	1.3	-1.0	0.2	0.3	0.6
Saint Kitts and Nevis	4.4	1.5	2.8	-6.7	-4.4	0.5	-2.4	4.6	5.6	4.0
Saint Lucia	6.8	-0.9	1.3	-1.9	-2.9	-0.4	-1.9	-0.6	-0.3	0.6
Saint Vincent and the Grenadines	7.5	-1.7	6.6	-2.2	-3.4	-0.4	1.4	1.7	0.6	0.9
Suriname	10.5	4.1	3.0	1.8	4.0	4.2	2.1	1.9	0.9	1.3
Trinidad and Tobago	13.9	4.0	2.9	-4.8	2.8	-0.8	0.8	1.8	-1.5	-0.2

Source: Economic Commission for Latin America and the Caribbean (ECLAC), on the basis of official figures.
[a] Preliminary figures.
[b] Based on official figures expressed in dollars at constant 2010 prices.

Table A.4
Latin America and the Caribbean: gross fixed capital formation [a]
(Percentages of GDP)

	2006	2007	2008	2009	2010	2011	2012	2013	2014	2015 [b]
Latin America and the Caribbean	18.4	19.4	20.6	19.5	20.4	21.3	21.3	21.5	20.8	19.7
Argentina	17.2	18.1	18.9	16.1	18.0	19.8	18.3	18.3	17.2	17.3
Bahamas	29.0	27.9	25.8	25.4	24.0	25.3	26.8	25.9	27.3	...
Belize	19.6	20.0	24.9	20.1	15.3	14.9	15.7	18.1	...	...
Bolivia (Plurinational State of)	13.4	14.4	16.1	16.1	16.6	19.5	19.0	19.9	20.7	20.5
Brazil	16.8	17.8	19.1	18.8	20.5	21.1	20.6	21.3	20.3	18.5
Chile	18.3	19.4	22.4	19.9	21.0	22.8	24.1	23.6	21.8	21.5
Colombia	19.6	21.0	22.3	21.7	21.9	24.4	24.6	24.8	26.3	26.4
Costa Rica	18.6	20.3	22.0	19.7	19.8	20.7	21.2	23.0	23.2	23.9
Cuba	10.0	9.6	9.9	9.1	8.6	8.8	9.1	9.4	...	...
Dominican Republic	25.3	26.3	27.1	22.9	25.0	23.4	22.3	21.3	21.9	22.8
Ecuador	21.8	22.1	24.1	23.1	24.6	26.1	27.3	28.9	29.4	29.2
El Salvador	16.3	16.9	15.8	13.2	13.3	14.8	14.3	15.4	14.1	0.0
Guatemala	20.0	19.7	18.0	15.6	14.8	15.2	15.3	15.0	15.0	15.2
Haiti	25.2	25.1	25.6	25.7	25.4	26.4	27.2	27.7	27.5	...
Honduras	27.9	32.7	33.3	22.1	21.6	24.3	24.2	23.1	22.1	21.3
Mexico	21.7	22.3	23.1	22.0	21.2	21.9	22.1	21.5	21.6	21.9
Nicaragua	22.0	23.8	23.9	19.4	21.4	24.4	27.7	27.9	26.4	27.8
Panama	21.9	27.5	29.5	28.2	30.2	33.7	37.3	42.2	43.7	...
Paraguay	12.9	13.7	15.2	14.7	15.9	16.9	15.8	15.5	16.0	16.3
Peru	16.5	18.7	21.9	20.9	23.5	24.3	26.3	26.1	25.0	25.3
Uruguay	17.2	17.6	19.6	17.7	19.1	19.4	22.3	22.1	21.9	21.4
Venezuela (Bolivarian Republic of)	18.5	21.3	20.7	19.6	18.7	18.7	21.9	20.7	16.8	...

Source: Economic Commission for Latin America and the Caribbean (ECLAC), on the basis of official figures.
[a] Based on official figures expressed in dollars at constant 2010 prices.
[b] Preliminary figures.

Table A.5
Latin America and the Caribbean: balance of payments
(Millions of dollars)

	Exports of goods f.o.b.			Exports of services			Imports of goods f.o.b.			Imports of services		
	2013	2014	2015[a]	2013	2014	2015[a]	2013	2014	2015[a]	2013	2014	2015[a]
Latin America and the Caribbean	1 115 607	1 082 067	...	151 448	153 194	...	1 105 370	1 091 150	...	228 168	230 269	...
Latin America[b]	1 006 496	990 781	875 990	136 243	139 314	136 479	1 027 869	1 027 322	931 447	197 547	202 865	186 781
Argentina	81 660	71 977	60 460	14 834	14 021	13 988	70 541	62 520	56 543	18 604	17 165	17 091
Bolivia (Plurinational State of)	11 657	12 266	8 463	1 104	1 242	1 367	9 338	10 518	9 688	1 731	2 341	2 161
Brazil	241 507	224 098	188 991	38 150	39 965	34 477	241 189	230 627	175 484	84 383	88 072	73 311
Chile	76 477	75 675	64 160	12 452	10 967	9 741	74 657	67 908	58 401	15 855	14 724	14 080
Colombia	60 281	57 000	37 388	6 859	6 846	6 862	57 101	61 610	53 391	12 784	13 505	11 560
Costa Rica	8 665	9 139	7 763	6 551	6 808	6 749	14 433	14 814	13 360	2 061	2 200	2 110
Dominican Republic	9 424	9 920	9 519	6 449	7 044	7 562	16 801	17 288	16 302	2 761	2 818	3 105
Ecuador	25 686	26 604	19 155	2 029	2 334	2 403	26 178	26 672	21 871	3 525	3 556	3 259
El Salvador	4 334	4 256	4 464	2 087	2 226	2 400	9 629	9 463	9 453	1 470	1 487	1 458
Guatemala	10 183	10 994	11 180	2 570	2 750	2 819	16 359	17 052	16 736	2 651	2 886	3 071
Haiti	915	961	1 023	652	701	728	3 329	3 660	3 426	1 090	1 075	991
Honduras	7 805	8 072	8 448	1 013	1 087	1 122	10 953	11 070	11 631	1 681	1 784	1 837
Mexico	380 729	397 866	382 986	20 194	21 086	22 903	381 638	400 440	400 860	31 177	33 537	34 850
Nicaragua	3 292	3 622	3 406	1 325	1 388	1 393	5 802	6 024	6 039	1 071	960	1 050
Panama	17 159	15 338	15 151	9 828	10 758	11 698	24 125	23 468	21 835	4 780	4 774	4 773
Paraguay	13 605	13 116	11 301	849	892	830	11 942	12 079	10 249	1 068	1 114	1 071
Peru	42 861	39 533	33 104	5 814	5 874	6 265	42 248	40 809	36 728	7 615	7 674	8 002
Uruguay	10 257	10 347	9 027	3 482	3 324	3 172	11 608	11 302	9 451	3 241	3 192	3 002
Venezuela (Bolivarian Republic of)	88 962	74 000	...	2 208	1 780	...	53 023	42 000	...	19 830	17 834	...
The Caribbean	20 148	17 285	444	12 997	12 100	1 743	24 478	21 829	2 118	10 791	9 569	838
Antigua and Barbuda	68	55	55	482	498	509	503	500	500	218	225	239
Bahamas	955	849	...	2 671	2 716	...	3 166	3 270	...	1 628	1 720	...
Barbados	...	...	...	...	...	...	...	...	...	...	...	...
Belize	608	589	...	448	494	...	876	926	...	208	225	...
Dominica	41	41	42	134	137	150	179	181	186	65	68	70
Grenada	45	46	46	169	192	202	324	299	293	100	98	100
Guyana	1 376	...	...	165	...	...	1 847	...	...	500	...	...
Jamaica	1 580	1 453	...	2 666	2 826	...	5 462	5 184	...	2 048	2 160	...
Saint Kitts and Nevis	56	62	64	253	266	300	252	278	297	128	135	149
Saint Lucia	200	182	181	408	445	446	546	522	517	190	184	185
Saint Vincent and the Grenadines	54	54	56	127	129	135	327	319	326	92	92	95
Suriname	2 395	2 149	...	172	203	...	2 126	1 966	...	584	782	...
Trinidad and Tobago	12 770	11 806	...	5 302	4 193	...	8 871	8 386	...	5 030	3 880	...

Table A.5 (continued)

	Goods and services balance			Income balance			Current transfers balance			Current account balance		
	2013	2014	2015[a]	2013	2014	2015[a]	2013	2014	2015[a]	2013	2014	2015[a]
Latin America and the Caribbean	-66 672	-84 013	...	-151 985	-158 827	...	62 481	65 201	...	-156 176	-178 387	...
Latin America[b]	-82 677	-100 092	-105 758	-136 790	-145 750	-125 878	60 836	62 943	64 778	-158 631	-182 898	-166 858
Argentina	7 350	6 312	815	-11 026	-12 020	-12 193	-892	-169	-207	-4 568	-5 877	-11 585
Bolivia (Plurinational State of)	1 692	649	-2 018	-1 908	-1 707	-1 480	1 270	1 084	980	1 054	26	-2 518
Brazil	-45 914	-54 636	-25 327	-32 538	-52 170	-45 000	3 683	2 729	2 310	-74 769	-104 076	-68 017
Chile	-1 582	4 010	1 421	-10 730	-8 857	-6 040	2 187	1 851	1 555	-10 125	-2 995	-3 064
Colombia	-2 745	-11 268	-20 701	-14 216	-12 670	-7 000	4 594	4 358	5 011	-12 367	-19 580	-22 690
Costa Rica	-1 277	-1 068	-958	-1 498	-1 378	-1 661	269	284	229	-2 505	-2 162	-2 390
Dominican Republic	-3 689	-3 143	-2 326	-2 994	-3 209	-2 624	4 147	4 326	4 620	-2 537	-2 026	-330
Ecuador	-1 989	-1 289	-3 572	-1 378	-1 565	-1 612	2 399	2 264	2 005	-968	-590	-3 179
El Salvador	-4 677	-4 468	-4 047	-997	-1 050	-1 126	4 100	4 318	4 295	-1 574	-1 199	-878
Guatemala	-6 257	-6 195	-5 807	-1 207	-1 638	-1 372	6 113	6 446	6 825	-1 351	-1 387	-354
Haiti	-2 853	-3 073	-2 666	32	12	12	2 283	2 291	2 436	-537	-769	-218
Honduras	-3 815	-3 695	-3 897	-1 353	-1 322	-1 314	3 405	3 572	3 861	-1 763	-1 444	-1 351
Mexico	-11 893	-15 024	-29 821	-39 440	-31 927	-30 432	21 653	22 915	24 519	-29 680	-24 036	-35 733
Nicaragua	-2 256	-1 973	-2 289	-313	-308	-332	1 369	1 443	1 444	-1 200	-838	-1 177
Panama	-1 918	-2 146	241	-3 064	-3 232	-3 300	63	120	233	-4 920	-5 258	-2 826
Paraguay	1 443	814	811	-1 685	-1 537	-1 498	720	606	605	477	-117	-82
Peru	-1 188	-3 077	-5 361	-10 631	-9 328	-6 777	3 346	4 374	3 937	-8 474	-8 031	-8 201
Uruguay	-1 110	-823	-255	-1 843	-1 845	-2 130	129	129	120	-2 825	-2 538	-2 265
Venezuela (Bolivarian Republic of)	18 317	18 248	...	-11 788	-9 620	...	-1 202	-300	...	5 327	7 580	...
The Caribbean	-2 313	-2 170	-769	-3 407	-3 457	-144	2 847	2 558	137	-2 873	-3 068	-776
Antigua and Barbuda	-171	-172	-175	-31	-37	-42	26	29	29	-176	-181	-189
Bahamas	-1 168	-1 424	...	-329	-437	...	3	0	...	-1 494	-1 860	...
Barbados	-189	-157	...	-195	-197	...	-13	-15	...	-397	-369	...
Belize	-28	-67	...	-118	-143	...	73	74	...	-73	-136	...
Dominica	-68	-70	-63	-20	-19	-19	20	21	21	-68	-68	-61
Grenada	-210	-159	-144	-30	-35	-30	18	26	21	-221	-168	-154
Guyana	-807	...	...	38	...	...	344	...	...	-426	...	...
Jamaica	-3 263	-3 065	...	-277	-386	...	2 221	2 292	...	-1 320	-1 160	...
Saint Kitts and Nevis	-71	-84	-82	-23	-28	-29	45	45	44	-49	-67	-67
Saint Lucia	-128	-78	-75	-26	-26	-21	5	10	10	-150	-94	-86
Saint Vincent and the Grenadines	-236	-229	-229	0	0	-2	14	13	13	-223	-216	-218
Suriname	-142	-396	...	-122	-61	...	67	71	...	-198	-386	...
Trinidad and Tobago	4 170	3 733	...	-2 276	-2 088	...	25	-8	...	1 920	1 637	...

Table A.5 (concluded)

	Capital and financial balance [c]			Overall balance			Reserve assets (variation) [d]			Other financing		
	2013	2014	2015 [a]	2013	2014	2015 [a]	2013	2014	2015 [a]	2013	2014	2015 [a]
Latin America and the Caribbean	172 078	216 726	...	19 405	38 339	...	-19 708	-37 389	...	303	-950	...
Latin America [b]	178 542	220 013	138 830	19 911	37 115	-28 028	-20 183	-36 293	28 028	272	-822	11
Argentina	-7 256	7 072	7 020	-11 824	1 195	-4 566	11 824	-1 195	4 566	0	0	0
Bolivia (Plurinational State of)	67	944	1 363	1 122	971	-1 156	-1 122	-971	1 156	0	0	0
Brazil	68 843	114 909	63 664	-5 926	10 833	-4 353	5 926	-10 833	4 353	0	0	0
Chile	10 436	4 052	1 211	311	1 057	-1 854	-311	-1 057	1 854	0	0	0
Colombia	19 314	24 017	22 192	6 946	4 437	-498	-6 946	-4 437	498	0	0	0
Costa Rica	2 966	2 048	3 088	461	-113	699	-461	113	-699	0	0	0
Dominican Republic	3 877	2 640	167	1 341	614	-162	-1 146	-162	162	-195	-453	0
Ecuador	2 814	165	2 491	1 846	-424	-687	-1 878	411	687	32	13	0
El Salvador	1 248	1 167	958	-327	-33	80	327	33	-80	0	0	0
Guatemala	2 053	1 459	585	702	73	231	-702	-73	-231	0	0	0
Haiti	178	675	72	-359	-94	-146	-58	479	146	418	-385	11
Honduras	2 235	1 904	1 580	473	459	229	-485	-459	-229	12	-1	0
Mexico	47 468	40 365	21 980	17 789	16 329	-13 753	-17 789	-16 329	13 753	0	0	0
Nicaragua	1 295	1 120	1 324	96	282	148	-96	-282	-148	0	0	0
Panama	5 320	6 480	2 914	401	1 222	88	-401	-1 222	-88	0	0	0
Paraguay	558	1 255	-579	1 036	1 138	-661	-1 036	-1 131	661	0	-7	0
Peru	11 376	5 843	8 061	2 902	-2 188	-140	-2 907	2 178	140	5	10	0
Uruguay	5 748	3 898	738	2 923	1 360	-1 527	-2 923	-1 360	1 527	0	0	0
Venezuela (Bolivarian Republic of)	-9 827	-8 708	...	-996	-1 128	...	996	1 128	...	0	0	...
The Caribbean	3 363	5 420	776	490	2 352	...	-522	-2 223	...	31	-129	...
Antigua and Barbuda	218	275	189	42	94	...	-42	-94	...	0	0	...
Bahamas	1 425	1 906	...	-69	46	...	69	-46	...	0	0	...
Barbados	240	323	...	-157	-46	...	157	46	...	0	0	...
Belize	190	221	...	117	85	...	-114	-84	...	-4	-1	...
Dominica	61	86	61	-6	18	...	6	-18	...	0	0	...
Grenada	253	191	154	31	23	...	-31	-23	...	0	0	...
Guyana	475	...	...	49	0	...	-84	0	...	34	0	...
Jamaica	1 140	1 960	...	-179	800	...	179	-673	...	0	-128	...
Saint Kitts and Nevis	89	130	67	40	62	...	-40	-62	...	0	0	...
Saint Lucia	110	161	86	-40	67	...	40	-67	...	0	0	...
Saint Vincent and the Grenadines	249	239	218	26	23	...	-26	-23	...	0	0	...
Suriname	47	236	...	-151	-150	...	151	150	...	0	0	...
Trinidad and Tobago	-1 133	-307	...	786	1 330	...	-786	-1 330	...	0	0	...

Source: Economic Commission for Latin America and the Caribbean (ECLAC), on the basis of official figures.
[a] Preliminary figures.
[b] Does not include the Bolivarian Republic of Venezuela.
[c] Includes errors and omissions.
[d] A minus sign (-) indicates an increase in reserve assets.

Table A.6
Latin America and the Caribbean: international trade of goods
(Indices: 2010=100)

| | Exports of goods, f.o.b. | | | | | | | | |
| | Value | | | Volume | | | Unit value | | |
	2013	2014	2015[a]	2013	2014	2015[a]	2013	2014	2015[a]
Latin America	125.5	122.0	105.3	111.0	113.4	115.4	113.0	107.6	91.3
Argentina	119.8	105.6	88.7	100.0	90.1	87.0	119.7	117.2	102.0
Bolivia (Plurinational State of)	182.1	191.6	132.2	148.0	162.2	151.5	123.1	118.1	87.3
Brazil	120.0	111.3	93.9	106.3	104.2	107.3	112.9	106.9	87.5
Chile	107.5	106.4	90.2	108.8	110.8	109.1	98.8	96.0	82.7
Colombia	147.9	139.8	91.7	131.0	139.0	128.4	112.9	100.6	71.4
Costa Rica	115.1	121.4	103.1	114.0	121.0	108.2	100.9	100.3	95.3
Dominican Republic	138.3	145.6	139.7	135.3	144.0	145.2	102.2	101.1	96.2
Ecuador	141.6	146.7	105.6	115.8	123.1	128.5	122.3	119.1	82.2
El Salvador	124.8	122.5	128.5	118.6	114.3	123.6	105.2	107.2	104.0
Guatemala	119.3	128.8	131.0	117.4	129.3	139.9	101.6	99.6	93.6
Haiti	162.4	170.6	181.6	152.3	156.9	166.1	106.6	108.7	109.3
Honduras	124.6	128.9	134.9	125.9	130.2	145.6	98.9	98.9	92.6
Mexico	127.4	133.1	128.1	113.4	124.0	130.5	112.4	107.4	98.2
Nicaragua	135.7	149.4	140.5	132.0	145.2	142.3	102.8	102.8	98.7
Panama	135.2	120.9	119.4	126.6	113.1	113.3	106.9	106.9	105.4
Paraguay	129.9	125.2	107.9	115.3	112.4	104.1	112.6	111.4	103.6
Peru	119.7	110.4	92.5	106.8	105.8	103.5	112.1	104.4	89.3
Uruguay	127.7	128.8	112.4	106.9	108.3	103.8	119.5	119.0	108.3
Venezuela (Bolivarian Republic of)	135.3	112.6	...	103.3	92.7	...	130.9	121.4	...

| | Imports of goods, f.o.b. | | | | | | | | |
| | Value | | | Volume | | | Unit value | | |
	2013	2014	2015[a]	2013	2014	2015[a]	2013	2014	2015[a]
Latin America	131.3	129.9	116.3	119.5	119.3	114.9	109.9	108.9	101.2
Argentina	130.2	115.4	104.4	117.3	103.8	100.7	111.0	111.2	103.7
Bolivia (Plurinational State of)	167.0	188.1	173.3	153.1	175.1	177.1	109.1	107.5	97.9
Brazil	131.9	126.1	96.0	116.0	113.2	94.9	113.7	111.5	101.1
Chile	135.3	123.1	105.9	126.2	116.7	112.8	107.2	105.5	93.9
Colombia	148.7	160.4	139.0	132.8	147.0	140.0	112.0	109.1	99.3
Costa Rica	131.4	134.9	121.7	125.1	130.3	127.3	105.1	103.5	95.6
Dominican Republic	110.5	113.7	107.2	98.9	104.9	114.1	111.7	108.4	94.0
Ecuador	133.3	135.8	111.4	123.3	128.7	112.2	108.1	105.5	99.2
El Salvador	128.5	126.3	126.1	117.5	117.2	130.3	109.3	107.7	96.8
Guatemala	127.7	133.2	130.7	115.4	123.4	134.6	110.7	107.9	97.1
Haiti	110.6	121.6	113.8	83.6	92.9	97.2	132.3	130.9	117.1
Honduras	123.0	124.3	130.6	110.1	113.6	131.0	111.7	109.4	99.7
Mexico	126.5	132.7	132.8	118.1	123.0	128.3	107.1	107.8	103.5
Nicaragua	133.4	138.5	138.8	119.9	129.7	148.3	111.2	106.8	93.6
Panama	140.1	136.3	126.8	128.1	127.2	123.4	109.4	107.2	103.0
Paraguay	124.5	125.9	106.8	113.6	116.7	110.8	109.6	107.9	96.4
Peru	146.6	141.6	127.5	129.5	127.0	127.9	113.2	111.5	99.7
Uruguay	135.6	132.1	110.4	116.8	118.5	112.6	116.1	111.4	98.1
Venezuela (Bolivarian Republic of)	137.6	109.0	...	125.0	100.4	...	110.1	108.5	...

Source: Economic Commission for Latin America and the Caribbean (ECLAC), on the basis of official figures.
[a] Estimates.

Table A.7
Latin America: terms of trade for goods f.o.b. / f.o.b.
(Indices: 2010=100)

	2006	2007	2008	2009	2010	2011	2012	2013	2014	2015[a]
Latin America	91.5	94.1	97.2	89.7	100.0	108.0	105.3	102.9	98.8	90.2
Argentina	81.0	86.0	96.4	97.2	100.0	111.3	115.8	107.8	105.4	98.4
Bolivia (Plurinational State of)	88.7	90.1	91.3	88.4	100.0	111.0	114.8	112.8	109.9	89.2
Brazil	83.5	85.2	88.3	86.2	100.0	107.9	101.6	99.3	95.9	86.6
Chile	89.8	92.9	80.8	81.7	100.0	100.6	94.9	92.2	91.0	88.2
Colombia	82.4	86.4	91.5	86.2	100.0	114.6	108.4	100.9	92.2	71.9
Costa Rica	105.7	104.7	100.8	104.1	100.0	96.3	95.8	96.1	97.0	99.7
Dominican Republic	97.3	100.5	96.0	103.8	100.0	94.7	93.8	91.5	93.3	102.4
Ecuador	91.0	93.5	102.6	90.8	100.0	110.0	111.7	113.1	112.9	82.9
El Salvador	104.5	103.5	100.6	103.9	100.0	100.0	96.6	96.2	99.6	107.5
Guatemala	96.9	95.1	92.6	100.5	100.0	99.1	93.7	91.8	92.3	96.4
Haiti	114.4	111.2	79.9	103.4	100.0	83.0	86.0	80.6	83.1	93.4
Honduras	98.8	97.0	91.1	97.3	100.0	108.4	94.6	88.6	90.4	92.9
Mexico	102.9	103.8	104.6	92.9	100.0	107.2	105.0	104.9	99.6	94.9
Nicaragua	95.4	94.5	90.4	99.1	100.0	99.6	99.6	92.4	96.3	105.5
Panama	102.9	101.9	97.3	101.9	100.0	97.8	98.2	97.7	99.7	102.3
Paraguay	91.0	95.3	102.3	100.0	100.0	102.4	103.4	102.8	103.3	107.5
Peru	89.8	94.0	84.7	82.9	100.0	107.2	105.0	99.0	93.6	89.6
Uruguay	87.4	87.4	94.4	100.9	100.0	102.9	106.7	102.9	106.8	110.4
Venezuela (Bolivarian Republic of)	85.4	93.6	115.5	84.1	100.0	120.2	121.4	118.9	111.8	...

Source: Economic Commission for Latin America and the Caribbean (ECLAC), on the basis of official figures.
[a] Estimates.

Table A.8
Latin America and the Caribbean (selected countries): remittances from emigrant workers
(Millions of dollars)

	2006	2007	2008	2009	2010	2011	2012	2013	2014	2015[a]
Bolivia (Plurinational State of)	569	1 020	1 097	1 023	939	1 012	1 094	1 182	1 164	670[b]
Brazil[c]	2 890	2 809	2 913	2 224	2 518	2 550	2 191	2 124	2 128	2 064
Colombia	3 861	4 430	4 785	4 090	3 996	4 064	3 970	4 401	4 093	3 776
Costa Rica	490	596	584	489	505	487	527	561	559	250[b]
Dominican Republic[c]	...	...	...	...	3 683	4 008	4 045	4 262	4 571	2 490[b]
Ecuador[c]	...	3 335	3 083	2 736	2 591	2 672	2 467	2 450	2 462	1 126[b]
El Salvador	3 471	3 695	3 742	3 387	3 455	3 628	3 894	3 940	4 154	3 519
Guatemala	3 610	4 128	4 315	3 912	4 127	4 378	4 783	5 105	5 544	5 178
Honduras	2 252	2 510	2 707	2 403	2 526	2 750	2 842	3 093	3 437	3 081
Jamaica	1 770	1 964	2 021	1 792	1 906	2 025	2 037	2 065	2 157	1 283[d]
Mexico	25 567	26 059	25 145	21 306	21 304	22 803	22 438	21 892	23 647	20 700
Nicaragua	698	740	818	768	823	912	1 014	1 078	1 136	977
Paraguay	101	198	202	201	274	451	528	519	422	321[e]
Peru	1 837	2 131	2 444	2 409	2 534	2 697	2 788	2 707	2 639	2 003[e]

Source: Economic Commission for Latin America and the Caribbean (ECLAC), on the basis of official figures.
[a] Figures as of October.
[b] Figures as of June.
[c] New methodology according to the sixth edition of the Balance of Payments Manual of the International Monetary Fund (IMF).
[d] Figures as of July.
[e] Figures as of September.

Table A.9
Latin America and the Caribbean: net resource transfer [a]
(Millions of dollars)

	2006	2007	2008	2009	2010	2011	2012	2013	2014	2015 [b]
Latin America and the Caribbean	-93 726	16 080	-31 366	-23 132	28 007	39 498	24 141	20 395	56 949	...
Latin America [c]	-66 151	36 776	-6 541	-6 017	54 267	76 914	48 330	42 023	73 442	13 902
Argentina	-10 388	-198	-14 317	-15 947	-8 304	-16 239	-14 889	-18 282	-4 948	-5 173
Bolivia (Plurinational State of)	-175	-43	-154	-1 094	-707	923	-1 888	-1 840	-762	-118
Brazil	-10 553	56 642	-9 401	37 269	57 805	65 132	38 651	36 304	62 739	18 664
Chile	-23 481	-29 153	-1 352	-13 265	-15 432	3 358	-2 016	-294	-4 805	-4 830
Colombia	-2 896	2 776	-669	-2 857	576	-2 047	1 665	5 097	11 347	15 192
Costa Rica	2 058	1 929	2 022	-22	762	1 192	3 058	1 469	671	1 427
Cuba	-618	-960	...	...	...	...	...	...	...	...
Dominican Republic	-221	665	2 462	1 248	3 167	2 522	1 079	688	-1 022	-2 456
Ecuador	-3 691	-2 138	-2 246	-2 264	-625	-522	-1 614	1 468	-1 387	880
El Salvador	375	1 040	1 477	179	-302	79	1 025	251	117	-168
Guatemala	1 096	1 159	809	-902	29	154	511	846	-179	-787
Haiti	573	688	374	373	969	573	788	627	303	95
Honduras	149	612	1 530	-429	546	521	32	894	581	266
Mexico	-9 698	2 423	8 201	-1 921	12 579	21 204	8 679	8 028	8 438	-8 451
Nicaragua	802	1 124	1 316	895	761	993	777	983	812	993
Panama	-648	710	1 565	-715	1 077	2 921	1 668	2 257	3 248	553
Paraguay	-1 101	-1 046	-915	-767	-1 036	-603	-1 184	-1 127	-289	-2 076
Peru	-7 681	-165	-288	-6 728	3 531	-5 495	7 644	749	-3 475	1 284
Uruguay	-52	710	3 045	929	-1 131	2 248	4 343	3 905	2 053	-1 393
Venezuela (Bolivarian Republic of)	-23 103	-19 031	-22 386	-16 054	-23 176	-35 543	-22 060	-21 615	-18 328	...
The Caribbean	-4 472	-1 665	-2 438	-1 061	-3 085	-1 874	-2 129	-13	1 835	632
Antigua and Barbuda	260	333	292	108	146	88	136	187	238	147
Bahamas	787	723	903	909	627	992	1 162	1 096	1 469	...
Barbados	74	235	137	187	120	270	203	45	126	...
Belize	-51	-84	38	22	-88	-60	-32	68	77	...
Dominica	48	66	108	118	72	64	79	42	67	42
Grenada	203	211	201	160	154	177	157	223	156	124
Guyana	137	137	235	-51	9	341	311	547	...	...
Jamaica	798	937	2 120	430	871	1 326	433	864	1 446	...
Saint Kitts and Nevis	70	89	183	172	142	143	66	66	102	38
Saint Lucia	268	295	257	125	195	231	158	84	135	65
Saint Vincent and the Grenadines	106	168	204	189	221	163	208	249	239	216
Suriname	-211	-181	-96	-68	-720	-389	-175	-75	175	...
Trinidad and Tobago	-6 962	-4 594	-7 022	-3 362	-4 833	-5 220	-4 835	-3 409	-2 395	...

Source: Economic Commission for Latin America and the Caribbean (ECLAC), on the basis of official figures.
[a] The net resource transfer is calculated as total net capital income minus the income balance (net payments of profits and interest). Total net capital income is the balance on the capital and financial accounts plus errors and omissions, plus loans and the use of IMF credit plus exceptional financing. Negative figures indicate resources transferred outside the country.
[b] Preliminary figures.
[c] Does not include the Bolivarian Republic of Venezuela.

Table A.10
Latin America and the Caribbean: net foreign direct investment [a]
(Millions of dollars)

	2006	2007	2008	2009	2010	2011	2012	2013	2014	2015
Latin America and the Caribbean	34 284	94 429	102 462	70 955	111 930	145 362	148 979	148 079	139 257	...
Latin America	30 995	90 601	96 718	68 007	109 432	142 219	145 754	145 966	137 251	...
Argentina	3 099	4 969	8 335	3 306	10 368	9 352	14 269	10 411	2 793	...
Bolivia (Plurinational State of)	278	363	509	420	651	859	1 060	1 750	648	...
Brazil	-9 380	27 518	24 601	36 033	61 689	85 091	81 399	54 240	70 855	...
Chile	6 586	8 326	7 453	6 159	6 049	3 057	7 902	8 956	9 950	...
Colombia	5 558	8 136	8 110	3 789	947	6 228	15 646	8 557	12 252	...
Costa Rica	1 371	1 634	2 072	1 223	1 378	2 216	1 944	2 481	1 954	...
Dominican Republic	1 085	1 667	2 870	2 165	1 622	2 277	3 142	1 990	2 209	...
Ecuador	271	194	1 058	308	165	644	567	732	773	...
El Salvador	267	1 455	824	366	-226	218	484	176	274	...
Guatemala	552	720	737	574	782	1 009	1 205	1 262	1 365	...
Haiti	161	75	30	55	178	119	156	160	99	...
Honduras	669	926	1 007	505	971	1 012	851	992	1 120	...
Mexico	15 248	24 145	27 640	8 160	11 151	10 726	-2 739	32 032	16 837	...
Nicaragua	266	366	608	463	474	930	715	708	800	...
Panama	2 557	1 777	2 207	1 259	2 407	2 977	3 279	4 373	4 351	...
Paraguay	114	202	209	95	216	557	738	72	424	...
Peru	3 467	5 425	6 188	6 020	8 189	7 518	11 840	9 161	7 789	...
Uruguay	1 495	1 240	2 117	1 512	2 349	2 511	2 539	3 027	2 761	...
Venezuela (Bolivarian Republic of)	-2 666	1 462	143	-4 405	73	4 919	756	4 888	...	...
The Caribbean	3 289	3 828	5 744	2 948	2 497	3 143	3 225	2 113	2 005	...
Antigua and Barbuda	359	338	159	81	97	65	133	95	161	...
Bahamas	706	746	860	664	872	667	526	388	259	...
Barbados	298	394	470	303	344	750	426	...	...	...
Belize	108	139	167	108	96	95	193	92	138	...
Dominica	26	40	57	42	24	14	29	24	33	...
Grenada	90	157	135	103	60	43	31	113	40	...
Guyana	102	152	168	164	198	247	278	201	...	...
Jamaica	797	751	1 361	480	169	144	411	741	701	...
Saint Kitts and Nevis	110	134	178	131	116	110	108	136	118	...
Saint Lucia	234	272	161	146	121	81	74	92	73	...
Saint Vincent and the Grenadines	109	119	159	110	97	86	115	160	138	...
Suriname	-163	-247	-231	-93	-248	73	128	138	4	...
Trinidad and Tobago	513	830	2 101	709	549	771	772	-66	339	...

Source: Economic Commission for Latin America and the Caribbean (ECLAC), on the basis of official figures.
[a] Corresponds to direct investment in the reporting economy after deduction of outward direct investment by residents of that country. Includes reinvestment of profits.

Table A.11
Latin America and the Caribbean: gross external debt
(Millions of dollars, end-of-period stocks)

		2006	2007	2008	2009	2010	2011	2012	2013	2014	2015 [a]
Latin America and the Caribbean [b]		663 265	736 827	769 325	829 735	990 557	1 112 503	1 214 888	1 282 533	1 401 356	1 429 810
Latin America		650 568	723 872	755 883	815 404	973 803	1 094 801	1 197 365	1 263 733	1 381 630	1 410 371
Argentina	Total	109 504	125 366	125 859	116 622	130 843	142 492	143 336	140 795	143 321	149 458
Bolivia (Plurinational State of)	Total	6 278	5 403	5 930	5 801	5 875	6 298	6 711	7 756	8 543	8 860
Brazil	Total	172 621	193 159	198 492	198 136	256 804	298 204	327 590	312 517	352 684	350 321
Chile	Total	48 601	53 627	63 534	72 617	84 986	99 306	120 546	132 632	145 666	148 716
Colombia	Total	40 103	44 553	46 369	53 719	64 723	75 903	78 763	91 923	101 212	108 199
Costa Rica	Total	7 191	8 444	9 105	8 238	9 579	11 131	14 717	17 513	19 433	21 046
Dominican Republic	Public	6 295	6 556	7 219	8 215	9 947	11 625	12 872	14 919	16 074	15 708
Ecuador	Total	17 099	17 445	16 900	13 514	13 914	15 210	15 913	18 801	24 133	27 169
El Salvador	Total	9 692	9 349	9 994	9 882	9 698	10 670	12 521	13 238	14 177	14 124
Guatemala	Total	9 844	10 909	11 163	11 248	12 026	14 021	15 339	17 307	19 054	19 682
Haiti	Public	1 484	1 627	1 921	1 333	354	709	1 173	1 562	1 827	1 827
Honduras	Total	3 935	3 190	3 499	3 365	3 785	4 208	4 861	6 709	7 180	7 145
Mexico	Total	119 788	125 494	124 007	160 787	193 950	208 972	223 733	254 793	282 479	291 029
Nicaragua	Public	4 527	3 385	3 512	3 661	4 068	4 263	4 481	4 724	4 796	4 735
Panama	Public	7 788	8 276	8 477	10 150	10 439	10 858	10 782	12 231	14 352	15 040
Paraguay	Total	2 618	2 731	3 124	3 044	3 621	3 864	4 580	5 112	6 307	6 398
Peru	Total	28 387	33 239	34 997	35 157	43 674	47 977	59 376	60 823	64 512	63 789
Uruguay	Total	12 977	14 864	15 425	17 969	18 425	18 345	21 122	22 862	24 166	25 411
Venezuela (Bolivarian Republic of)	Total	41 835	56 256	66 358	81 946	97 092	110 745	118 949	127 515	131 715	131 715
The Caribbean	Public	12 696	12 955	13 442	14 331	16 755	17 702	17 523	18 800	19 726	19 439
Antigua and Barbuda	Public	321	481	436	416	432	467	445	525	526	552
Bahamas	Public	289	273	384	703	728	799	1 038	1 188	1 555	1 604
Barbados	Public	958	997	989	1 198	1 359	1 382	1 325	1 436	1 492	1 392
Belize	Public	985	973	958	1 017	1 021	1 032	1 029	1 083	1 126	1 160
Dominica	Public	225	241	234	222	232	237	262	273	278	278
Grenada	Public	481	469	481	512	528	535	535	562	574	601
Guyana	Public	1 043	718	834	933	1 043	1 206	1 358	1 246	1 216	1 233
Jamaica	Public	5 796	6 123	6 344	6 594	8 390	8 626	8 256	8 310	8 659	8 285
Saint Kitts and Nevis	Public	335	323	312	325	296	320	317	320	283	268
Saint Lucia	Public	365	399	364	373	393	417	435	488	541	520
Saint Vincent and the Grenadines	Public	187	219	229	262	313	328	329	354	381	364
Suriname	Public	391	298	319	269	334	463	567	739	810	889
Trinidad and Tobago	Public	1 322	1 443	1 557	1 507	1 686	1 891	1 627	2 276	2 284	2 293

Source: Economic Commission for Latin America and the Caribbean (ECLAC), on the basis of official figures.
[a] Preliminary figures.
[b] Includes debt owed to the International Monetary Fund.

Table A.12

Latin America and the Caribbean: sovereign spreads on EMBI+ and EMBI Global

(Basis points to end of period)

		2006	2007	2008	2009	2010	2011	2012	2013	2014	2015 [a]
Latin America	EMBI+	186	268	722	328	305	410	317	410	491	549
Argentina	EMBI+	216	410	1 704	660	496	925	991	808	719	487
Belize	EMBI Global	...	...	...	...	617	1 391	2 245	807	819	800
Bolivia (Plurinational State of)	EMBI Global	...	...	...	...	...	...	...	289	277	259
Brazil	EMBI+	192	221	428	192	189	223	142	224	259	432
Chile	EMBI Global	84	151	343	95	115	172	116	148	169	235
Colombia	EMBI+	161	195	498	196	172	195	112	166	196	289
Dominican Republic	EMBI Global	...	...	...	...	322	597	343	349	381	405
Ecuador	EMBI Global	920	614	4 731	769	913	846	826	530	883	1 207
El Salvador	EMBI Global	...	...	...	...	302	478	396	389	414	591
Jamaica	EMBI Global	...	...	...	...	427	637	711	641	485	441
Mexico	EMBI+	98	149	376	164	149	187	126	155	182	218
Panama	EMBI+	148	184	540	171	162	201	129	199	189	212
Paraguay	EMBI Global	...	...	...	...	...	...	...	240	291	325
Peru	EMBI+	118	178	509	165	163	216	114	159	181	229
Uruguay	EMBI Global	185	243	685	238	188	213	127	194	208	266
Venezuela (Bolivarian Republic of)	EMBI+	182	506	1 862	1 017	1 044	1 197	773	1 093	2 295	2 535

Source: Economic Commission for Latin America and the Caribbean (ECLAC), on the basis of information from JPMorgan, Emerging Markets Bond Index Monitor.
[a] Figures as of November.

Table A.13

**Latin America and the Caribbean: sovereign risk premiums
on five-year credit default swaps**

(Basis points to end of period)

	2006	2007	2008	2009	2010	2011	2012	2013	2014	2015 [a]
Argentina	203	462	4 041	914	602	922	1 442	1 654	2 987	...
Brazil	100	103	301	123	111	162	108	194	201	444
Chile	19	32	203	68	84	132	72	80	94	126
Colombia	114	130	309	143	113	156	96	119	141	222
Mexico	40	69	293	134	114	154	98	92	103	155
Panama	80	118	302	134	99	150	98	111	109	169
Peru	91	116	304	124	113	172	97	133	115	181
Venezuela (Bolivarian Republic of)	129	452	3 218	1 104	1 016	928	647	1 150	3 155	3 940

Source: Economic Commission for Latin America and the Caribbean (ECLAC), on the basis of information from Bloomberg.
[a] Figures as of November.

Table A.14
Latin America and the Caribbean: international bond issues [a]
(Millions of dollars)

	2006	2007	2008	2009	2010	2011	2012	2013	2014	2015 [b]
Total	45 224	41 515	19 848	64 750	90 183	91 687	114 241	123 332	133 056	79 445
National issues	44 407	40 976	19 401	63 250	88 657	90 272	111 757	121 518	129 743	75 661
Argentina	1 896	3 256	65	500	3 146	2 449	663	1 025	1 941	3 486
Bahamas	-	-	100	300	-	-	-	-	300	
Barbados	215	-	-	450	390	-	-	-	2 500	320
Bolivia (Plurinational State of)	-	-	-	-	-	-	500	500	-	-
Brazil	18 989	10 608	6 520	25 745	39 305	38 369	50 255	37 262	45 364	7 513
Chile	1 062	250	-	2 773	6 750	6 049	9 443	11 540	13 768	7 650
Colombia	3 427	3 065	1 000	5 450	1 912	6 411	7 459	10 012	9 200	6 400
Costa Rica	-	-	-	-	-	250	1 250	3 000	1 000	1 000
Dominican Republic	675	605	-	-	1 034	750	750	1 800	1 500	3 500
Ecuador	-	-	-	-	-	-	-	-	2 000	1 500
El Salvador	925	-	-	800	450	654	800	310	800	300
Guatemala	-	-	30	-	-	150	1 400	1 300	1 100	-
Honduras	-	-	-	-	20	-	-	1 000	-	-
Jamaica	930	1 900	350	750	1 075	694	1 750	1 800	1 800	2 925
Mexico	9 200	10 296	6 000	16 659	26 882	22 276	28 147	41 729	37 592	30 075
Panama	2 076	670	686	1 323	-	897	1 100	1 350	1 935	1 700
Paraguay	-	-	-	-	-	100	500	500	1 000	280
Peru	733	1 827	-	2 150	4 693	2 155	7 240	5 840	5 944	6 407
Trinidad and Tobago	500	-	-	850	-	175	-	550	-	-
Uruguay	3 679	999	-	500	-	1 693	500	2 000	2 000	2 605
Venezuela (Bolivarian Republic of)	100	7 500	4 650	5 000	3 000	7 200	-	-	-	-
Supranational issues	817	539	447	1 500	1 526	1 415	2 484	1 814	3 313	3 785
Central American Bank for Economic Integration (CABEI)	183	-	-	500	151	-	250	520	505	385
Caribbean Development Bank (CDB)	-	-	-	-	-	175	-	-	-	-
Foreign Trade Bank of Latin America (BLADEX)	-	-	-	-	-	-	400	-	-	-
Development Bank of Latin America (CAF)	634	539	447	1 000	1 375	1 240	1 834	1 294	2 808	2 650
Sable International Finance	-	-	-	-	-	-	-	-	-	750

Source: Economic Commission for Latin America and the Caribbean (ECLAC), on the basis of figures provided by Merrill-Lynch, JP Morgan and LatinFinance.
[a] Includes sovereign, bank and corporate bonds.
[b] Figures as of November.

Table A.15
Latin America and the Caribbean: stock exchange indices
(National indices to end of period, 31 December 2005=100)

	2006	2007	2008	2009	2010	2011	2012	2013	2014	2015 [a]
Argentina	135	139	70	150	228	160	185	349	556	841
Brazil	133	191	112	205	207	170	182	154	149	135
Chile	137	155	121	182	251	213	219	188	196	186
Colombia	117	112	79	122	163	133	155	137	122	88
Costa Rica	177	217	207	142	118	121	129	190	211	190
Ecuador	130	121	128	107	126	128	135	148	168	160
Jamaica	96	103	77	80	82	91	88	77	73	128
Mexico	149	166	126	180	217	208	246	240	242	244
Peru	268	365	147	295	487	406	430	328	308	213
Trinidad and Tobago	91	92	79	72	78	95	100	111	108	108
Venezuela (Bolivarian Republic of)	256	186	172	270	320	574	2 312	13 421	18 925	63 533

Source: Economic Commission for Latin America and the Caribbean (ECLAC), on the basis of information from Bloomberg.
[a] Figures as of November.

Table A.16
Latin America and the Caribbean: gross international reserves
(Millions of dollars, end-of-period stocks)

	2006	2007	2008	2009	2010	2011	2012	2013	2014	2015 [a]
Latin America and the Caribbean	319 340	459 581	512 727	567 444	655 389	773 631	835 735	830 009	857 437	824 795
Latin America	309 687	448 480	498 906	553 531	639 515	756 687	820 026	813 974	839 356	807 544
Argentina	31 167	45 711	46 198	47 967	52 145	46 376	43 290	30 599	31 443	26 970
Bolivia (Plurinational State of)	3 193	5 319	7 722	8 580	9 730	12 018	13 927	14 430	15 123	13 967
Brazil	85 839	180 334	193 783	238 520	288 575	352 012	373 147	358 808	363 551	361 230
Chile	19 429	16 910	23 162	25 373	27 864	41 979	41 650	41 094	40 447	38 593
Colombia	15 440	20 955	24 041	25 365	28 464	32 303	37 474	43 639	47 328	46 830
Costa Rica [b]	3 115	4 114	3 799	4 066	4 627	4 756	6 857	7 331	7 211	7 910
Dominican Republic [b]	2 251	2 946	2 662	3 307	3 765	4 098	3 559	4 701	4 862	4 699
Ecuador [c]	2 023	3 521	4 473	3 792	2 622	2 958	2 483	4 361	3 949	3 308
El Salvador	1 907	2 197	2 544	2 985	2 882	2 503	3 175	2 745	2 693	2 774
Guatemala [b]	4 061	4 320	4 659	5 213	5 954	6 188	6 694	7 273	7 333	7 564
Haiti	305	494	587	733	1 284	1 344	1 337	1 690	1 163	871 [d]
Honduras [b]	2 824	2 733	2 690	2 174	2 775	2 880	2 629	3 113	3 570	3 799 [e]
Mexico	76 330	87 211	95 302	99 893	120 587	149 209	167 050	180 200	195 682	181 929 [f]
Nicaragua	862	1 032	1 062	1 490	1 708	1 793	1 778	1 874	2 147	2 309
Panama [b]	1 379	2 094	2 637	3 222	2 561	2 234	2 441	2 775	3 994	4 082 [f]
Paraguay	1 703	2 462	2 864	3 861	4 168	4 984	4 994	5 871	6 891	6 336
Peru	17 329	27 720	31 233	33 175	44 150	48 859	64 049	65 710	62 353	62 213
Uruguay	3 091	4 121	6 360	7 987	7 743	10 302	13 605	16 281	17 555	17 113
Venezuela (Bolivarian Republic of)	37 440	34 286	43 127	35 830	27 911	29 892	29 890	21 481	22 061	15 045
The Caribbean	9 653	11 101	13 821	13 913	15 874	16 944	15 709	16 034	18 081	17 251
Antigua and Barbuda [g]	143	144	138	108	136	147	161	202	297	278 [h]
Bahamas	500	454	563	816	861	892	812	740	787	827 [f]
Barbados	444	622	523	563	575	587	630	516	467	458 [f]
Belize	95	99	156	210	216	242	289	402	482	433 [f]
Dominica [g]	63	60	55	64	66	75	92	85	100	106 [h]
Grenada [g]	100	110	104	112	103	106	104	135	158	158 [h]
Guyana	277	313	356	628	780	798	862	777	666	611 [f]
Jamaica	2 399	1 906	1 795	1 752	2 979	2 820	1 981	1 818	2 473	2 895
Saint Kitts and Nevis [g]	89	96	110	123	156	233	252	291	318	317 [h]
Saint Lucia [g]	132	151	140	151	182	192	208	168	235	309 [h]
Saint Vincent and the Grenadines [g]	78	86	83	75	111	88	109	133	156	148 [h]
Suriname	215	401	433	659	639	941	1 008	779	625	398 [f]
Trinidad and Tobago	5 118	6 659	9 364	8 652	9 070	9 823	9 201	9 987	11 317	10 312 [f]

Source: Economic Commission for Latin America and the Caribbean (ECLAC), on the basis of official figures.
[a] Figures as of November.
[b] Series corresponding to the harmonized monetary and financial statistics.
[c] Freely available International reserves.
[d] Figures as of July.
[e] Figures as of August.
[f] Figures as of September.
[g] Net international reserves.
[h] Figures as of March.

Table A.17

Latin America and the Caribbean: real effective exchange rates [a]

(Indices: 2005=100, average values for the period)

	2006	2007	2008	2009	2010	2011	2012	2013	2014 [b]	2015 [b c]
Latin America and the Caribbean [d]	97.4	94.7	89.3	88.3	85.6	83.5	81.3	81.3	83.3	83.7
Barbados	96.1	97.3	93.9	88.8	85.8	82.6	79.9	79.8	79.4	77.6
Bolivia (Plurinational State of)	96.6	91.8	79.7	73.7	75.7	74.3	70.3	66.5	63.2	57.3
Brazil	88.4	81.5	77.7	79.5	68.6	65.4	72.7	77.6	80.4	96.2
Chile	94.3	95.0	93.2	98.0	91.4	89.8	88.6	90.4	100.4	103.4
Colombia	100.6	88.5	83.0	86.3	76.2	76.0	72.7	76.7	80.8	99.0
Costa Rica	98.9	95.9	91.4	91.4	80.2	77.3	74.3	71.6	74.8	71.4
Dominica	100.5	102.1	100.2	98.6	97.8	99.8	98.5	99.7	100.4	99.0
Dominican Republic	105.4	103.4	103.4	105.0	103.3	103.0	103.9	107.6	110.0	109.5
Ecuador	100.5	103.5	101.4	95.0	93.5	95.3	90.9	91.1	88.9	81.9
El Salvador	99.4	99.1	97.5	95.9	96.5	95.9	95.5	96.5	96.7	95.5
Guatemala	96.5	95.3	88.9	93.0	90.4	86.0	84.6	83.1	80.1	75.6
Honduras	98.0	96.1	91.2	85.1	83.4	82.4	80.7	81.4	79.1	78.9
Jamaica	100.8	101.8	93.1	100.6	90.5	87.0	84.7	88.5	91.7	89.9
Mexico	99.8	100.2	102.2	116.7	107.5	107.2	110.6	105.1	106.6	119.8
Nicaragua	98.6	98.6	90.5	92.7	94.4	97.2	94.2	94.0	93.9	91.2
Panama	101.1	102.2	99.6	96.0	97.0	97.0	89.7	88.1	87.0	83.5
Paraguay	86.3	76.3	66.7	74.0	70.0	60.6	62.7	60.8	60.0	61.7
Peru	100.5	100.1	95.8	94.6	90.7	92.4	85.7	86.5	88.7	90.5
Trinidad and Tobago	95.7	92.8	87.6	80.6	74.7	74.7	69.1	66.7	63.7	59.0
Uruguay	95.9	92.9	85.2	81.3	69.5	65.7	65.4	62.3	65.7	66.9
Venezuela (Bolivarian Republic of)	92.8	81.7	65.8	51.1	76.7	67.0	56.4	58.2	...	...

Source: Economic Commission for Latin America and the Caribbean (ECLAC), on the basis of official figures.

[a] Annual averages. A country's overall real effective exchange rate index is calculated by weighting its real bilateral exchange rate indices with each of its trading partners by each partner's share in the country's total trade flows in terms of exports and imports. The extraregional real effective exchange rate index excludes trade with other Latin American and Caribbean countries. A currency depreciates in real effective terms when this index rises and appreciates when it falls.

[b] Preliminary figures.

[c] Figures as of October.

[d] Simple average of the extraregional real effective exchange rate for 21 countries. As from 2014, does not include the Bolivarian Republic of Venezuela.

Table A.18
Latin America and the Caribbean: participation rate
(Average annual rates)

		2006	2007	2008	2009	2010	2011	2012	2013	2014	2014 January to September	2015 [a] January to September
Latin America and the Caribbean [b]		59.2	59.4	59.4	59.6	59.8	60.0	60.2	60.0	59.5	...	...
Argentina	Urban areas	60.3	59.5	58.8	59.3	58.9	59.5	59.3	58.9	58.3	58.1	57.7
Bahamas	Nationwide total	...	...	...	73.4	...	72.3	74.6	73.2	73.7	...	...
Barbados	Nationwide total	67.9	67.8	67.6	67.0	66.6	67.6	66.2	66.7	63.8	63.9	64.8 [c]
Belize	Nationwide total	57.6	61.2	59.2	...	...	...	65.8	64.5 [d]	...	...	...
Bolivia (Plurinational State of)	Departamental capitals [e]	58.7	57.1	...|	56.9	57.3 [f]	...	...	...	...	...	...
Brazil	Six metropolitan areas [g]	56.9	56.9	57.0	56.7	57.1	57.1	57.3	57.1	56.0	61.1	61.2
Chile [h]	Nationwide total	54.8	54.9	56.0	55.9		58.5	59.8	59.5	59.6	59.8	59.7	59.6
Colombia	Nationwide total	59.1	58.3	58.5	61.3	62.7	63.7	64.5	64.2	64.2	64.1	64.6 [i]
Costa Rica [j]	Nationwide total	56.6	57.0	56.7		60.4	59.1	60.7	60.1	59.8	59.5	62.8	61.7 [k]
Cuba [l]	Nationwide total	72.1	73.7	74.7	75.4	74.9	76.1	74.2	72.9	71.9	...	...
Dominican Republic	Nationwide total	56.0	56.1	55.6	53.8	55.0	56.2	56.5	56.1	57.3		...	...
Ecuador	Urban total [g]	64.9	67.8	67.7	66.3	64.2	62.2	62.8	61.8	62.2	62.7	66.3
El Salvador [m]	Nationwide total	52.6|	62.1	62.7	62.8	62.5	62.7	63.2	63.6	62.8	...	...
Guatemala [n]	Nationwide total	...	60.1	...	...	54.3		61.8	65.4	60.6	60.9	...	...
Honduras	Nationwide total	50.7	50.7	51.0	53.1	53.6	51.9	50.8	53.7	56.0	56.0	58.3 [o]
Jamaica	Nationwide total	64.7	64.9	65.4	63.5	62.4	62.3	61.9	63.0	62.8	62.8	63.0
Mexico	Nationwide total	58.7	58.8	58.7	58.6	58.4	58.6	59.2	60.3	59.8	59.9	59.6
Nicaragua [j]	Nationwide total	51.4	53.4	53.3		51.8	71.4	77.0	76.8	75.8	74.2	...	...
Panama	Nationwide total	62.6	62.7	63.9	64.1	63.5	61.9	63.4	64.1	64.0	64.0	64.2 [p]
Paraguay	Nationwide total	59.4	60.8	61.7	62.9	60.5	60.7	64.3	62.6	61.6	...	...
Peru	Metropolitan Lima	67.4	68.9	68.1	68.4	70.0	70.0	69.1	68.9	68.4	68.4	68.0
Trinidad and Tobago	Nationwide total	63.9	63.5	63.5	62.7	62.1	61.3	61.8	61.3	61.9	62.6	60.8 [q]
Uruguay	Nationwide total	60.7	62.5	62.7	63.4	62.9	64.8	64.0	63.6	64.7	64.5	63.7
Venezuela (Bolivarian Republic of)	Nationwide total	65.4	64.9	64.9	65.1	64.6	64.4	63.9	64.3	65.3	...	...

Source: Economic Commission for Latin America and the Caribbean (ECLAC), on the basis of official figures.
[a] The figures in the last two columns refer to the period January-September.
[b] The regional series are weighted averages of national data (excluding the Bahamas, Belize, Guatemala, Nicaragua and the Plurinational State of Bolivia) and include adjustments for lack of information and changes in methodology. The data relating to the different countries are not comparable owing to differences in coverage and in the definition of the working-age population.
[c] The figures in the last two columns refer to the period January-June.
[d] The figures refer to the measurement for April.
[e] Up to 2007, urban areas.
[f] First semester.
[g] The figures in the last two columns refer to nationwide total.
[h] New measurements have been used since 2010; the data are not comparable with the previous series.
[i] The figures in the last two columns refer to the period January-October.
[j] New measurements have been used since 2009; the data are not comparable with the previous series.
[k] The figures in the last two columns refer to a new measurement; the data are not comparable with the previous series.
[l] The working-age population is measured as follows: for males, 17 to 59 years and for females, 15 to 54 years.
[m] New measurements have been used since 2007; the data are not comparable with the previous series.
[n] New measurements have been used since 2011; the data are not comparable with the previous series.
[o] The figures in the last two columns refer to the measurement for June.
[p] The figures in the last two columns refer to the measurement for August.
[q] The figures in the last two columns refer to the measurement for March.

Table A.19
Latin America and the Caribbean: open urban unemployment [a]
(Average annual rates)

		2006	2007	2008	2009	2010	2011	2012	2013	2014	2015 [b]
Latin America and the Caribbean [c]		8.6	7.9	7.3	8.1	7.3	6.7	6.4	6.2	6.0	6.6
Argentina	Urban areas	10.2	8.5	7.9	8.7	7.7	7.2	7.2	7.1	7.3	6.3 [d]
Bahamas [e]	Nationwide total	7.6	7.9	8.7	14.2	…	15.9	14.4	15.8	14.8	12.0 [f]
Barbados [e]	Nationwide total	8.7	7.4	8.1	10.0	10.8	11.2	11.6	11.6	12.3	11.9 [g]
Belize [e]	Nationwide total	9.4	8.5	8.2	13.1	12.5	…	15.3	13.2	11.6	10.1 [h]
Bolivia (Plurinational State of)	Departamental capitals [i]	8.0	7.7	6.7	7.9	6.1	5.8	…	…	…	…
Brazil	Six metropolitan areas	10.0	9.3	7.9	8.1	6.7	6.0	5.5	5.4	4.8	6.9
Chile	Nationwide total	7.7	7.1	7.8	9.7	8.2	7.1	6.4	5.9	6.4	6.3
Colombia [e]	Thirteen metropolitan areas	13.1	11.4	11.5	13.0	12.4	11.5	11.2	10.6	9.9	9.6
Colombia [j]	Thirteen metropolitan areas	12.2	10.7	11.0	12.4	11.8	10.9	10.6	10.1	9.5	9.2
Costa Rica [k]	Urban total	6.0	4.8	4.8	8.5	7.1	7.7	9.8	9.1	9.5	9.6
Cuba	Nationwide total	1.9	1.8	1.6	1.7	2.5	3.2	3.5	3.3	2.7	…
Dominican Republic	Nationwide total	5.5	5.0	4.7	5.3	5.0	5.8	6.5	7.0	6.4	…
Ecuador [e]	Urban total	8.1	7.4	6.9	8.5	7.6	6.0	4.9	4.7	5.1	5.3 [d]
Ecuador [j]	Urban total	5.7	5.5	5.4	6.9	6.1	5.0	4.2	4.0	4.3	4.7 [d]
El Salvador	Urban total	5.7	5.8	5.5	7.1	6.8	6.6	6.2	5.6	6.7	…
Guatemala [l]	Urban total	…	…	…	…	4.8	3.1	4.0	3.8	4.0	…
Honduras	Urban total	4.9	4.0	4.1	4.9	6.4	6.8	5.6	6.0	7.5	8.8
Jamaica [e]	Nationwide total	10.3	9.8	10.6	11.4	12.4	12.6	13.9	15.2	13.7	13.5 [m]
Jamaica [j]	Nationwide total	5.8	6.0	6.9	7.5	8.0	8.4	9.3	10.3	9.4	9.6 [m]
Mexico	Urban areas	4.6	4.8	4.9	6.6	6.4	5.9	5.8	5.7	5.8	5.1
Nicaragua	Urban total	7.0	5.9	6.1	8.2	7.8	5.9	5.9	5.7	6.8	…
Panama [e]	Urban total	10.4	7.8	6.5	7.9	7.7	5.4	4.8	4.7	5.4	5.8
Panama [j]	Urban total	8.4	5.8	5.0	6.3	5.8	3.6	3.6	3.7	4.1	4.5
Paraguay	Asuncion and urban areas of the Central Department [n]	8.9	7.2	7.4	8.2	7.2	7.1	8.1	8.1	8.0	7.2 [d]
Peru	Metropolitan Lima	8.5	8.4	8.4	8.4	7.9	7.7	6.8	5.9	6.0	6.5
Trinidad and Tobago [e]	Nationwide total	6.2	5.6	4.6	5.3	5.9	5.1	5.0	3.6	3.3	3.7 [o]
Uruguay	Urban total	11.4	9.8	8.3	8.2	7.5	6.6	6.7	6.7	6.9	7.9
Venezuela (Bolivarian Republic of) [e]	Nationwide total	9.9	8.4	7.3	7.9	8.7	8.3	8.1	7.8	7.0	…

Source: Economic Commission for Latin America and the Caribbean (ECLAC), on the basis of household surveys.
[a] Unemployed population as a percentage of the economically active population.
[b] Estimate based on data from January to October.
[c] Weighted average adjusted for lack of information and differences and changes in methodology. The data relating to the different countries are not comparable owing to differences in coverage and in the definition of the working age population.
[d] Estimate based on data from January to September.
[e] Includes hidden unemployment.
[f] Figures as of May.
[g] Figures as of first semester.
[h] Figures as of April.
[i] Up to 2007, urban areas.
[j] Includes an adjustment to the figures for the economically active population to exclude hidden unemployment.
[k] New measurements have been used since 2009; the data are not comparable with the previous series. New measurements have been used since 2012; the data are not comparable with the previous series.
[l] Owing to methodological changes, as of 2011 the data are not comparable with the previous series.
[m] January-July average.
[n] Up to 2011, urban total.
[o] Figures as of March.

Table A.20

Latin America and the Caribbean: employment rate [a]

(Average annual rates)

		2006	2007	2008	2009	2010	2011	2012	2013	2014	2014	2015 [b]
											January to September	
Latin America and the Caribbean [c]		54.2	55.0	55.3	55.1	55.7	56.1	56.6	56.5	56.2	...	...
Argentina	Urban areas	54.1	54.5	54.2	54.2	54.4	55.2	55.0	54.7	54.0	53.8	53.9
Bahamas	Nationwide total	69.4	70.2	69.7	63.0	...	60.6	64.1	61.6	62.7	...	...
Barbados	Nationwide total	61.9	62.7	62.1	60.3	59.4	60.0	58.5	58.9	56.0	56.0	57.5 [d]
Belize	Nationwide total	52.5	56.0	54.3	...	...	...	55.8	56.7 [e]	...	...	...
Bolivia (Plurinational State of)	Departamental capitals [f]	54.0	52.7		...	52.4	53.6 [g]	...	...	...	...	...	...
Brazil	Six metropolitan areas [h]	51.2	51.6	52.5	52.1	53.2	53.7	54.2	54.0	53.3	56.8	56.1
Chile [i]	Nationwide total	50.5	51.0	51.7	50.5		53.7	55.5	55.7	56.0	56.0	55.8	55.8
Colombia	Nationwide total	52.0	51.8	51.9	53.9	55.4	56.8	57.9	58.0	58.4	58.1	58.7 [j]
Costa Rica [k]	Nationwide total	53.3	54.4	53.9		55.4	54.8	56.0	55.4	54.7	54.5	56.8	55.7 [l]
Cuba [m]	Nationwide total	70.7	72.4	73.6	74.2	73.0	73.6	71.6	70.5	70.0	...	...
Dominican Republic	Nationwide total	46.9	47.4	47.7	45.8	47.1	48.0	48.2	47.7	49.0	...	...
Ecuador	Urban total [h]	61.2	56.8		63.1	60.7	59.3	58.5	59.7	58.9	59.0	59.9	63.5
El Salvador [n]	Nationwide total	49.2		58.1	59.0	59.2	58.1	58.6	59.4	59.9	58.4	...	...
Guatemala [o]	Nationwide total	...	58.6	...	...	...		59.2	63.5	58.7	59.1	...	...
Honduras	Nationwide total	49.0	49.2	49.4	51.5	51.5	49.7	48.9	51.6	53.1	53.1	54.0 [p]
Jamaica	Nationwide total	58.0	58.6	58.5	56.3		54.6	54.4	53.3	53.4	54.2	54.3	54.5
Mexico	Nationwide total	56.7	56.7	56.3	55.4	55.3	55.5	56.3	56.2	56.9	56.9	57.0
Nicaragua [k]	Nationwide total	48.8	48.6	50.1		61.8	66.8	...	...	...	69.2	...	...
Panama	Nationwide total	57.2	58.7	60.3	59.9	59.4	59.1	60.8	61.5	60.9	60.9	60.9 [q]
Paraguay	Nationwide total	55.4	57.4	57.0	57.1	57.1	57.3	61.2	59.4	57.9	...	...
Peru	Metropolitan Lima	61.8	63.0	62.4	62.7	64.5	64.5	64.4	64.8	64.3	64.2	63.4
Trinidad and Tobago	Nationwide total	59.9	59.9	60.6	59.4	58.4	58.2	58.8	59.1	59.9	60.6	58.6 [r]
Uruguay	Nationwide total	54.1	56.7	57.7	58.5	58.4	60.7	59.9	59.5	60.4	60.3	59.0
Venezuela (Bolivarian Republic of)	Nationwide total	58.9	59.5	60.2	60.0	59.0	59.0	58.7	59.3	60.4	...	...

Source: Economic Commission for Latin America and the Caribbean (ECLAC), on the basis of official figures.

[a] Employed population as a percentage of the working-age population.
[b] The figures in the last two columns refer to the period January-September.
[c] The regional series are weighted averages of national data (excluding the Bahamas, Belize, Guatemala, Nicaragua and the Plurinational State of Bolivia) and include adjustments for lack of information and changes in methodology. The data relating to the different countries are not comparable owing to differences in coverage and in the definition of the working age population.
[d] The figures in the last two columns refer to the period January-June.
[e] The figures refer to the measurement for April.
[f] Up to 2007, urban areas.
[g] First semester.
[h] The figures in the last two columns refer to Nationwide total.
[i] New measurements have been used since 2010; the data are not comparable with the previous series.
[j] The figures in the last two columns refer to the period January-October.
[k] New measurements have been used since 2009; the data are not comparable with the previous series.
[l] The figures in the last two columns refer to a new measurement; the data are not comparable with the previous series,
[m] The working-age population is measured as follows: for males, 17 to 59 years and for females, 15 to 54 years.
[n] New measurements have been used since 2007; the data are not comparable with the previous series.
[o] Owing to methodological changes, as of 2011 the data are not comparable with the previous series.
[p] The figures in the last two columns refer to the measurement for June.
[q] The figures in the last two columns refer to the measurement for August.
[r] The figures in the last two columns refer to the measurement for March.

Table A.21

Latin America: real average wages [a]

(Indices: 2010=100)

	2006	2007	2008	2009	2010	2011	2012	2013	2014	2015 [b]
Bolivia (Plurinational State of) [c]	109.2	102.2	94.4	96.5	100.0	98.2	99.3	100.3	100.9 [d]	...
Brazil [e]	93.4	94.3	96.3	98.5	100.0	101.4	104.9	107.1	108.8	105.4
Chile [f]	91.0	93.6	93.4	97.9	100.0	102.5	105.8	109.9	111.9	113.9
Colombia [g]	97.7	97.6	96.1	97.3	100.0	100.3	101.3	104.0	104.5	105.9
Costa Rica [h]	91.6	92.8	90.9	97.9	100.0	105.7	107.1	108.5	110.7	115.1
Cuba	93.9	92.5	92.6	96.2	100.0	98.8	97.7	98.0	119.8	...
El Salvador [i]	101.1	98.7	95.6	98.9	100.0	97.1	97.3	97.8	98.5	105.3
Guatemala [h]	101.3	99.7	97.1	97.2	100.0	100.4	104.4	104.3	106.8	...
Mexico [h]	100.3	101.7	101.9	100.9	100.0	100.8	101.0	100.9	101.3	102.8
Nicaragua [h]	99.3	97.2	93.3	98.8	100.0	100.1	100.5	100.7	102.4	105.2
Panama	93.6	94.7	90.9	93.3	100.0	100.1	103.5	103.8	109.5	109.8 [j]
Paraguay	93.5	95.7	95.0	99.4	100.0	102.8	103.5	105.7	107.1	107.1 [d]
Peru [k]	99.6	97.9	100.0	103.1	100.0	108.4	111.0	114.7	117.9	118.0
Uruguay	83.2	87.1	90.2	96.8	100.0	104.0	108.4	111.7	115.4	117.2
Venezuela (Bolivarian Republic of)	116.0	117.4	112.1	105.6	100.0	103.0	109.1	104.3	...	...

Source: Economic Commission for Latin America and the Caribbean (ECLAC), on the basis of official figures.
[a] Figures deflated by the official consumer price index of each country.
[b] Estimate based on data from January to September.
[c] Private-sector average wage index.
[d] Figure for June.
[e] Private-sector workers covered by social and labour legislation.
[f] General index of hourly remuneration.
[g] Manufacturing.
[h] Average wage declared by workers covered by social security.
[i] Average taxable wage.
[j] January-June average.
[k] Payroll workers in the Lima metropolitan area. Until 2010, formal private sector workers in the Lima metropolitan area.

Table A.22

Latin America and the Caribbean: monetary indicators

(Percentage variation with respect to the year-earlier period)

		2006	2007	2008	2009	2010	2011	2012	2013	2014	2015[a]
Latin America											
Argentina	Monetary base	23.7	29.0	19.1	5.4	25.1	37.1	34.9	30.2	19.7	31.8[b]
	Money (M1)	25.2	23.4	16.7	13.0	24.1	32.4	33.3	29.5	26.1	31.8[c]
	M2	22.4	24.5	18.1	5.9	27.6	36.9	32.4	30.9	23.1	32.6[c]
	Foreign-currency deposits	37.9	27.8	36.4	61.6	35.9	8.7	-22.6	-6.1	51.7	30.4[c]
Bolivia (Plurinational State of)	Monetary base	44.3	48.2	53.8	19.6	32.4	11.6	18.2	10.8	9.5	19.4
	Money (M1)	45.1	55.2	50.2	9.4	24.1	27.2	18.3	13.5	15.4	11.3[d]
	M2	53.6	68.1	59.6	18.4	34.6	34.0	31.3	22.6	18.8	18.8[d]
	Foreign-currency deposits	-2.8	11.2	-9.2	20.4	4.7	-12.8	-5.0	-4.1	-3.4	2.8[d]
Brazil	Monetary base	18.6	20.9	12.5	8.0	17.5	11.0	9.4	5.5	7.2	3.9[b]
	Money (M1)	15.4	23.3	11.8	7.4	17.5	6.1	5.9	10.7	4.7	-1.0[b]
	M2	15.6	14.1	30.3	22.1	11.1	21.0	13.4	9.3	11.7	6.9[b]
Chile	Monetary base	14.6	20.8	7.0	15.0	13.8	14.8	13.7	16.3	5.3	9.3
	Money (M1)	11.3	17.9	11.1	14.1	27.7	10.9	9.1	10.1	12.1	14.6
	M2	18.0	20.3	17.7	3.7	5.1	14.7	14.7	9.7	8.7	11.3
	Foreign-currency deposits	17.4	11.6	40.7	2.6	8.5	11.8	8.9	18.7	29.0	18.3
Colombia	Monetary base	23.2	18.1	14.3	10.3	12.4	15.1	9.5	12.5	16.7	14.3[b]
	Money (M1)	20.6	13.5	8.0	9.7	14.7	16.2	6.7	14.3	14.8	10.1[b]
	M2	18.0	18.7	14.6	13.2	6.9	14.8	16.9	17.5	12.9	9.7[b]
Costa Rica	Monetary base	30.2	25.4	25.7	6.3	10.0	11.7	12.1	14.1	11.7	11.0[b]
	Money (M1)	25.2	41.1	21.7	-3.4	9.5	19.2	9.4	11.9	13.0	7.7[c]
	M2	29.9	34.9	22.9	1.3	2.6	11.1	13.8	13.0	14.4	10.4[c]
	Foreign-currency deposits	17.0	7.2	10.7	36.8	-1.9	-7.1	-1.2	0.1	13.0	2.1[c]
Dominican Republic	Monetary base	13.2	18.4	12.3	3.4	6.4	5.8	9.0	3.9	3.3	22.5[b]
	Money (M1)	30.1	26.6	11.0	-1.1	17.5	4.9	7.3	12.1	13.6	12.7[b]
	M2	0.6	14.2	10.9	7.6	13.5	8.8	12.1	8.0	11.2	10.5[b]
	Foreign-currency deposits	17.1	10.7	15.0	4.4	18.9	17.8	18.4	16.1	11.5	11.2[b]
Ecuador	Monetary base	...	...	16.4	18.1	24.1	9.9	16.1	23.3	17.5	17.6[b]
	Money (M1)	...	...	44.5	38.0	16.1	15.5	14.0	14.8	14.4	13.0[c]
	M2	...	...	33.0	22.0	18.6	20.0	17.8	13.4	14.5	9.2[c]
El Salvador	Monetary base	7.1	13.9	8.1	10.8	0.4	-1.3	1.8	4.8	2.8	0.9[b]
	Money (M1)	12.6	12.2	8.5	7.6	19.8	10.4	4.4	2.9	4.0	3.6[b]
	M2	9.1	15.0	6.1	0.9	1.6	-2.1	0.5	1.8	0.8	3.2[b]
Guatemala	Monetary base	18.9	17.3	4.1	6.6	8.0	10.1	5.8	9.2	5.8	12.2[b]
	Money (M1)	17.9	17.6	3.4	7.6	7.2	9.1	5.8	7.0	5.2	12.2[b]
	M2	19.9	11.7	7.3	9.4	8.4	10.6	9.4	9.7	8.1	11.6[b]
	Foreign-currency deposits	6.1	4.2	9.9	18.1	11.6	4.9	3.2	11.2	9.4	6.4[b]
Haiti	Monetary base	12.4	11.3	16.1	14.2	34.1	18.1	9.2	0.4	-1.0	11.4[e]
	Money (M1)	8.8	3.5	21.4	9.2	26.9	14.4	8.7	11.1	8.7	17.5[e]
	M2	9.6	5.3	13.7	6.9	17.4	11.5	5.7	9.4	8.4	13.0[e]
	Foreign-currency deposits	15.9	3.2	22.1	14.4	22.5	18.4	6.9	8.2	8.5	13.5[e]
Honduras	Monetary base	14.9	31.3	24.8	11.6	-13.8	10.7	11.3	4.0	9.7	18.7[c]
	Money (M1)	22.0	18.4	11.5	2.2	5.2	17.7	2.1	-5.0	8.4	19.0[c]
	M2	26.5	19.4	9.2	0.8	4.7	17.2	8.7	3.6	8.9	13.1[c]
	Foreign-currency deposits	12.7	10.5	20.3	-1.0	5.4	7.8	15.3	12.6	7.3	13.5[c]

Table A.22 (continued)

		2006	2007	2008	2009	2010	2011	2012	2013	2014	2015 [a]
Mexico	Monetary base	16.5	12.6	12.6	15.9	9.7	9.5	13.9	6.3	13.5	20.7 [b]
	Money (M1)	35.9	11.6	8.5	11.8	11.2	16.2	13.7	7.5	13.9	16.7 [b]
	M2	19.8	7.5	13.9	11.5	5.8	12.4	10.7	7.1	11.0	13.8 [b]
	Foreign-currency deposits	24.9	-6.4	2.8	20.7	0.9	3.0	16.8	13.3	26.6	39.6 [b]
Nicaragua	Monetary base	25.5	18.3	15.2	0.7	24.0	20.5	18.3	6.3	12.9	16.0 [b]
	Money (M1)	18.8	18.2	32.9	4.4	21.4	24.8	17.6	8.5	16.5	19.9 [d]
	M2	18.8	18.2	32.9	4.4	21.4	24.8	17.6	8.5	16.5	19.9 [d]
	Foreign-currency deposits	10.5	8.0	10.2	5.3	25.8	7.8	21.2	13.6	20.4	16.2 [d]
Panama	Monetary base	7.5	9.6	17.7	11.2	7.5	27.1	12.7	16.0	-1.2	31.2 [b]
	Money (M1)	24.5	29.2	26.5	17.4	19.2	21.5	17.1	6.9	13.6	1.4 [c]
	M2	14.8	22.4	17.1	9.2	11.3	9.9	10.8	6.3	12.4	6.2 [c]
Paraguay	Monetary base	8.7	31.2	27.6	30.7	5.2	5.0	11.8	5.1	8.3	13.0 [b]
	Money (M1)	16.5	34.4	30.5	6.6	28.7	7.8	8.6	15.6	9.6	13.1 [b]
	M2	12.9	34.2	38.4	13.3	26.4	14.0	13.7	17.4	10.6	12.3 [b]
	Foreign-currency deposits	0.9	9.3	21.1	40.1	16.4	13.5	14.9	15.8	29.3	21.3 [b]
Peru	Monetary base	17.1	25.2	38.2	2.1	24.2	31.3	31.2	21.1	-8.6	-0.6 [b]
	Money (M1)	17.1	30.6	31.3	8.8	28.0	19.9	18.9	14.0	4.5	5.8 [b]
	M2	7.7	37.7	48.5	-2.2	27.8	18.8	23.6	18.5	0.9	3.8 [b]
	Foreign-currency deposits	11.4	7.9	11.2	23.1	-0.1	14.1	0.2	16.0	20.3	14.4 [b]
Uruguay	Monetary base	23.5	28.9	28.6	6.1	12.9	23.1	21.8	15.3	11.0	11.6
	Money (M1)	28.5	23.0	22.4	13.1	24.6	19.6	18.4	11.7	6.1	6.9 [b]
	M2	28.8	22.5	26.1	11.3	25.8	26.0	17.4	12.4	8.7	9.1 [b]
	Foreign-currency deposits	5.9	2.2	3.1	24.1	2.3	10.7	19.6	14.8	25.8	25.4 [b]
Venezuela (Bolivarian Republic of)	Monetary base	61.7	65.5	39.5	18.3	24.5	27.0	40.8	61.1	86.5	89.2 [b]
	Money (M1)	105.5	66.8	24.3	28.8	27.5	44.8	62.0	66.1	69.5	80.9 [b]
	M2	61.9	60.2	16.9	28.3	18.0	37.6	57.5	65.4	69.1	80.7 [b]
The Caribbean											
Antigua and Barbuda	Monetary base	4.2	10.0	2.0	-10.5	0.9	20.1	29.4	13.2	20.0	18.3 [c]
	Money (M1)	10.8	16.4	6.7	-14.2	-7.3	-6.6	-2.1	3.1	11.5	3.0 [c]
	M2	7.2	11.3	7.6	-2.9	-3.1	-1.1	1.7	2.8	3.5	2.8 [c]
	Foreign-currency deposits	15.9	32.0	-0.5	39.9	-45.2	5.8	-12.8	0.9	20.0	8.2 [c]
Bahamas	Monetary base	-3.0	17.2	6.4	2.0	2.5	26.8	-7.8	2.2	13.8	-1.5 [f]
	Money (M1)	3.2	1.5	0.3	-0.2	2.8	6.2	8.6	5.6	8.4	23.2 [c]
	M2	7.1	8.5	6.5	2.8	2.8	2.3	1.1	-0.6	0.1	2.4 [c]
	Foreign-currency deposits	13.8	17.7	15.9	8.4	0.1	-2.7	11.6	15.8	-1.5	-14.8 [c]
Barbados	Monetary base	4.8	26.8	9.2	-13.9	3.4	7.7	-0.9	10.6	5.8	33.1 [c]
	Money (M1)	4.1	11.9	7.7	-5.3	1.7	-0.5	-20.3	5.5	9.4	11.3 [d]
	M2	11.0	11.7	9.3	-1.0	-0.8	0.3	-5.7	3.5	1.5	2.1 [d]
Belize	Monetary base	19.2	15.1	11.5	11.9	-1.2	8.2	17.5	19.2	18.8	24.5 [c]
	Money (M1)	13.0	17.0	9.2	-1.9	-0.9	9.1	24.0	13.7	14.0	14.6 [c]
Dominica	Monetary base	9.9	6.5	-0.1	-4.6	9.7	8.5	17.8	0.0	15.0	20.2 [c]
	Money (M1)	10.8	10.1	4.4	-1.3	-1.5	-2.1	9.8	2.5	2.2	8.2 [c]
	M2	6.7	10.5	8.2	7.5	3.8	3.2	7.0	4.5	6.5	4.5 [c]
	Foreign-currency deposits	-32.1	-0.6	19.0	15.9	30.2	38.8	25.4	-6.1	13.5	7.9 [c]

Table A.22 (concluded)

		2006	2007	2008	2009	2010	2011	2012	2013	2014	2015 [a]
Grenada	Monetary base	-11.1	9.2	3.5	-8.5	6.0	7.2	4.7	5.4	21.1	6.3 [c]
	Money (M1)	-5.8	7.1	3.1	-12.9	3.8	-7.3	2.9	5.4	24.1	22.5 [c]
	M2	-0.9	5.2	8.1	1.0	3.4	0.4	1.8	3.0	5.2	4.1 [c]
	Foreign-currency deposits	-18.7	26.0	2.7	17.4	-3.9	-5.5	5.5	-18.8	7.8	11.7 [c]
Guyana	Monetary base	4.2	0.8	16.5	10.6	17.7	17.4	15.2	6.6	2.5	15.0 [b]
	Money (M1)	14.2	20.5	18.6	8.2	12.9	21.9	16.1	6.7	10.1	9.7 [c]
Jamaica	Monetary base	14.2	15.1	9.5	22.8	5.5	5.3	6.3	6.3	5.9	9.4 [b]
	Money (M1)	17.2	18.8	9.1	7.6	7.0	7.8	4.7	5.9	5.0	14.7 [c]
	M2	11.8	14.3	7.9	4.4	6.1	5.6	3.3	6.4	2.6	9.0 [c]
	Foreign-currency deposits	3.0	18.2	10.9	17.5	-0.9	-4.8	6.8	28.5	9.2	14.2 [c]
Saint Kitts and Nevis	Monetary base	8.1	15.7	7.3	48.3	-3.2	36.1	13.7	22.2	10.5	-16.4 [c]
	Money (M1)	6.5	17.4	7.2	9.2	16.8	28.6	18.2	12.3	1.6	10.7 [c]
	M2	6.6	11.9	10.3	10.2	9.4	10.7	8.8	6.4	6.4	5.6 [c]
	Foreign-currency deposits	17.5	16.4	-9.2	-7.0	-9.0	-1.0	6.4	35.6	46.4	22.2 [c]
Saint Lucia	Monetary base	7.8	14.4	10.2	8.5	3.6	16.3	4.2	8.0	8.0	28.7 [c]
	Money (M1)	9.6	5.0	7.1	-2.4	-4.3	4.0	3.2	2.2	7.1	3.0 [c]
	M2	11.5	11.3	10.7	4.1	0.2	4.9	3.7	3.5	-1.0	1.4 [c]
	Foreign-currency deposits	32.5	47.8	8.9	9.3	-13.2	16.4	14.0	-10.1	45.0	15.6 [c]
Saint Vincent and the Grenadines	Monetary base	14.3	4.5	2.0	-3.2	11.9	0.8	11.8	26.2	16.9	7.7 [c]
	Money (M1)	12.8	6.8	-1.4	-8.3	-0.5	-3.9	-0.4	9.6	5.8	10.6 [c]
	M2	6.7	9.5	1.9	0.8	2.2	1.9	1.2	8.6	8.1	6.4 [c]
	Foreign-currency deposits	7.4	102.1	1.5	-6.5	-7.7	30.8	-7.3	29.2	15.6	16.2 [c]
Suriname	Monetary base	...	39.7	30.2	22.1	13.0	3.2	27.0	13.8	-7.2	-10.3 [b]
	Money (M1)	...	26.7	21.3	26.3	16.7	5.3	17.0	11.3	5.4	-6.8 [c]
	M2	...	30.2	21.0	25.1	18.2	7.0	20.0	17.7	8.1	-3.3 [c]
	Foreign-currency deposits	...	25.7	24.3	12.0	7.9	39.1	13.6	10.8	11.4	7.1 [c]
Trinidad and Tobago	Monetary base	41.5	19.0	32.3	37.6	24.7	14.1	15.4	19.5	8.0	-4.7 [c]
	Money (M1)	21.7	7.6	17.6	24.0	25.5	17.2	15.4	19.2	19.8	2.7 [c]
	M2	24.7	13.3	17.2	17.6	17.9	8.4	12.0	11.8	11.6	5.3 [c]
	Foreign-currency deposits	11.8	36.4	21.1	32.2	7.9	-4.0	4.7	12.6	-6.8	...

Source: Economic Commission for Latin America and the Caribbean (ECLAC), on the basis of official figures.
[a] Figures as of November.
[b] Figures as of October.
[c] Figures as of September.
[d] Figures as of August.
[e] Figures as of July.
[f] Figures as of June.

Table A.23
Latin America and the Caribbean: domestic credit
(Percentage variation with respect to the year-earlier period)

	2006	2007	2008	2009	2010	2011	2012	2013	2014	2015 [a]
Latin America										
Argentina	-6.2	1.7	23.9	2.3	51.3	59.5	33.0	40.8	24.7	34.6 [b]
Bolivia (Plurinational State of)	-3.2	6.5	7.5	10.9	13.0	18.8	22.7	21.6	17.6	15.5 [c]
Brazil	18.8	20.1	15.8	11.3	18.0	17.6	16.8	11.9	9.5	9.3
Chile	10.5	15.6	18.4	6.6	-0.1	12.1	15.1	9.3	7.6	7.6 [d]
Colombia	16.1	15.4	15.7	14.4	20.6	15.1	14.6	14.1	13.5	...
Costa Rica	16.6	22.1	21.1	19.1	4.6	12.4	11.7	9.2	19.9	13.6 [b]
Dominican Republic	22.6	10.7	17.4	12.3	7.5	9.5	12.1	12.4	11.6	14.3
Ecuador	9.3	18.2	1.7	20.8	33.6	31.5	21.5	16.7	16.2	12.0
El Salvador	8.6	12.4	11.3	2.4	2.2	3.5	9.6	5.5	9.5	6.8
Guatemala	15.5	13.8	10.4	5.2	5.6	15.2	11.3	12.6	12.0	12.2
Haiti	5.1	0.3	7.8	9.7	-23.0	-17.1	11.4	70.0	30.4	21.9 [d]
Honduras	34.4	49.0	27.1	6.7	10.0	10.8	18.0	9.6	6.8	8.0 [b]
Mexico	13.5	21.6	8.7	16.7	10.6	11.3	10.7	9.4	9.9	11.3 [d]
Nicaragua	4.4	11.4	16.7	-1.2	-4.6	-6.2	21.6	21.4	11.3	10.4 [b]
Panama	16.0	10.7	15.9	1.2	9.5	18.8	18.1	12.9	15.4	5.2 [b]
Paraguay	7.9	11.0	33.5	12.7	36.3	25.5	28.4	20.8	12.0	25.4
Peru	23.2	38.0	9.4	9.9	24.1	12.0	9.5	6.2	17.1	16.9
Uruguay	...	...	...	...	3.9	24.7	19.4	16.5	18.6	10.7
Venezuela (Bolivarian Republic of) [e]	82.7	51.6	22.0	28.4	13.7	36.0	56.1	61.9	63.8	61.9 [f]
The Caribbean										
Antigua and Barbuda	9.3	17.3	12.5	19.9	0.6	-3.8	-3.0	-4.9	-0.4	-5.1 [b]
Bahamas	14.3	4.8	7.5	5.3	3.4	0.8	4.0	1.9	0.0	1.4 [g]
Barbados	10.7	8.2	10.1	6.4	-0.5	-0.9	6.6	8.0	2.3	0.6 [h]
Belize	15.9	13.7	8.9	5.7	-0.4	-1.6	0.4	-2.6	-0.6	6.0 [b]
Dominica	3.7	-9.3	5.0	8.5	12.5	13.7	7.6	7.7	1.7	1.5 [b]
Grenada	12.5	15.4	13.1	8.9	3.9	2.6	5.0	-2.1	-9.0	-9.8 [b]
Guyana	-6.7	28.9	15.8	4.5	-0.8	34.5	40.1	26.3	16.0	10.2
Jamaica	-1.5	12.4	16.3	15.0	-3.4	-4.1	11.7	16.0	14.2	-2.0 [b]
Saint Kitts and Nevis	16.7	9.9	3.0	6.2	6.3	0.2	-9.0	-20.9	-18.7	-4.0 [b]
Saint Lucia	23.5	29.6	21.1	4.6	-0.3	2.9	6.6	5.4	-3.1	-13.0 [b]
Saint Vincent and the Grenadines	11.9	16.5	9.5	7.1	1.5	-7.2	-1.0	6.4	3.5	5.6 [b]
Suriname	...	20.7	18.5	16.9	21.4	20.8	10.3	23.5	21.5	20.9 [h]
Trinidad and Tobago	-40.0	90.1	6.5	35.5	36.6	9.3	7.9	-20.4	-23.8	-5.5 [b]

Source: Economic Commission for Latin America and the Caribbean (ECLAC), on the basis of official figures.
[a] Figures as of October.
[b] Figures as of September.
[c] Figures as of March.
[d] Figures as of July.
[e] Credit granted by commercial and universal banks.
[f] Figures as of May.
[g] Figures as of June.
[h] Figures as of August.

Table A.24
Latin America and the Caribbean: monetary policy rates
(Average rates)

	2006	2007	2008	2009	2010	2011	2012	2013	2014	2015 [a]
Latin America										
Argentina	7.3	9.1	11.3	14.0	12.3	11.8	12.8	14.6	26.7	26.2 [b]
Bolivia (Plurinational State of)	5.3	6.0	9.0	7.0	3.0	4.0	4.0	4.0	5.0	2.8 [c]
Brazil	15.4	12.0	12.4	10.1	9.9	11.8	8.6	8.3	11.0	13.4 [c]
Chile	5.0	5.3	7.2	1.8	1.5	4.8	5.0	4.9	3.7	3.0 [c]
Colombia	6.6	8.8	9.8	5.8	3.2	4.0	5.0	3.4	3.9	4.7
Costa Rica	8.8	6.0	8.0	9.6	8.1	5.6	5.0	4.5	4.9	3.8 [c]
Dominican Republic	9.2	7.3	9.0	5.1	4.2	6.4	5.9	5.2	6.3	5.4 [c]
Guatemala	4.7	5.5	6.9	5.5	4.5	4.9	5.3	5.1	4.6	3.4 [c]
Haiti	18.2	11.6	6.9	6.2	5.0	3.2	3.0	3.0	4.6	12.0 [c]
Honduras	6.4	6.3	8.4	4.9	4.5	4.8	6.6	7.0	7.0	6.5 [c]
Mexico	7.2	7.2	7.8	5.7	4.5	4.5	4.5	4.0	3.2	3.0 [c]
Paraguay	9.7	6.0	5.9	2.1	2.2	7.9	6.0	5.5	6.7	6.2 [c]
Peru	4.3	4.7	5.9	3.3	2.1	4.0	4.3	4.2	3.8	3.3 [c]
Uruguay [d]	...	...	7.4	8.5	6.3	7.5	8.8	9.3	...	...
Venezuela (Bolivarian Republic of)	9.8	9.8	12.3	8.1	6.3	6.4	6.4	6.2	6.4	6.1 [b]
The Caribbean										
Antigua and Barbuda	6.5	6.5	6.5	6.5	6.5	6.5	6.5	6.5	6.5	6.5 [c]
Bahamas	5.3	5.3	5.3	5.3	5.3	4.8	4.5	4.5	4.5	4.5 [b]
Barbados	11.7	12.0	11.8	7.9	7.0	7.0	7.0	7.0	7.0	7.0 [e]
Belize	18.0	18.0	18.0	18.0	18.0	11.0	11.0	11.0	11.0	11.0 [f]
Dominica	6.5	6.5	6.5	6.5	6.5	6.5	6.5	6.5	6.5	6.5 [c]
Grenada	6.5	6.5	6.5	6.5	6.5	6.5	6.5	6.5	6.5	6.5 [c]
Guyana	6.4	6.5	6.6	6.9	6.4	5.4	5.4	5.0	5.0	5.0 [b]
Jamaica	12.3	11.7	14.1	14.8	9.0	6.6	6.3	5.8	5.8	5.6 [b]
Saint Kitts and Nevis	6.5	6.5	6.5	6.5	6.5	6.5	6.5	6.5	6.5	6.5 [c]
Saint Lucia	6.5	6.5	6.5	6.5	6.5	6.5	6.5	6.5	6.5	6.5 [c]
Saint Vincent and the Grenadines	6.5	6.5	6.5	6.5	6.5	6.5	6.5	6.5	6.5	6.5 [c]
Trinidad and Tobago	7.3	8.0	8.4	7.5	4.7	3.2	2.9	2.8	2.8	4.0

Source: Economic Commission for Latin America and the Caribbean (ECLAC), on the basis of official figures.
[a] Figures as of December.
[b] Figures as of October.
[c] Figures as of November.
[d] As from June 2013, interest rate no longer used as monetary policy tool.
[e] Figures as of September.
[f] Figures as of June.

Table A.25
Latin America and the Caribbean: representative lending rates
(Average rates)

	2006	2007	2008	2009	2010	2011	2012	2013	2014	2015 [a]
Latin America										
Argentina [b]	12.9	14.0	19.8	21.3	15.2	17.7	19.3	21.6	29.3	27.2 [c]
Bolivia (Plurinational State of) [d]	8.8	8.3	8.9	8.5	5.2	6.3	6.7	7.0	6.5	6.4
Brazil [e]	62.3	51.0	54.1	47.5	42.9	44.9	39.9	39.1	44.6	48.8 [c]
Chile [f]	14.4	13.6	15.2	12.9	11.8	12.4	13.5	13.2	10.8	9.4
Colombia [g]	12.9	15.4	17.2	13.0	9.4	11.2	12.6	11.0	10.9	11.3 [c]
Costa Rica [h]	22.7	17.3	16.7	21.6	19.8	18.1	19.7	17.4	16.6	15.9
Dominican Republic [i]	15.7	11.7	16.0	12.9	8.3	11.7	12.2	10.7	13.9	14.6 [c]
Ecuador [j]	8.9	10.1	9.8	9.2	9.0	8.3	8.2	8.2	8.1	8.2 [c]
El Salvador [k]	7.5	7.8	7.9	9.3	7.6	6.0	5.6	5.7	6.0	6.1 [c]
Guatemala [h]	12.8	12.8	13.4	13.8	13.3	13.4	13.5	13.6	13.8	13.2
Haiti [i]	29.5	31.2	23.3	21.6	20.7	19.8	19.4	18.9	18.6	18.5 [m]
Honduras [h]	17.4	16.6	17.9	19.4	18.9	18.6	18.4	20.1	20.6	20.8 [m]
Mexico [n]	...	...	...	...	...	29.9	28.6	27.9	28.6	28.6 [m]
Nicaragua [o]	11.6	13.0	13.2	14.0	13.3	10.8	12.0	15.0	13.5	12.1 [c]
Panama [p]	8.1	8.3	8.2	8.3	7.9	7.3	7.0	7.4	7.6	7.6 [c]
Paraguay [q]	15.7	12.8	13.5	14.6	12.5	16.9	16.6	16.6	15.7	14.1 [m]
Peru [f]	23.9	22.9	23.7	21.0	19.0	18.7	19.2	18.1	15.7	16.1
Uruguay [s]	10.7	10.0	13.1	16.6	12.0	11.0	12.0	13.3	17.2	16.9 [c]
Venezuela (Bolivarian Republic of) [t]	14.6	16.7	22.8	20.6	18.0	17.4	16.2	15.6	17.2	19.7 [c]
The Caribbean										
Antigua and Barbuda [i]	10.7	10.3	10.1	9.5	10.2	10.1	9.4	9.4	9.6	8.5 [m]
Bahamas [u]	10.0	10.6	11.0	10.6	11.0	11.0	10.9	11.2	11.8	12.3 [c]
Barbados [i]	10.7	10.7	10.4	9.8	9.5	9.3	8.6	8.5	8.6	8.6 [v]
Belize [w]	14.2	14.3	14.1	14.1	13.9	13.3	12.3	11.5	10.9	10.4 [m]
Dominica [i]	9.5	9.2	9.4	10.0	9.4	8.7	8.9	9.0	8.8	8.6 [m]
Grenada [i]	9.8	9.7	9.4	10.7	10.3	10.4	9.5	9.1	9.1	8.8 [c]
Guyana [i]	14.9	14.1	13.9	14.0	15.2	14.7	14.0	12.1	11.1	10.8 [c]
Jamaica [i]	22.0	22.0	22.3	22.6	20.3	18.3	17.8	16.3	15.1	15.0 [v]
Saint Kitts and Nevis [i]	9.2	9.3	8.6	8.6	8.5	9.2	8.5	8.4	8.8	8.5 [m]
Saint Lucia [i]	10.5	9.7	9.3	9.5	9.5	9.2	8.6	8.4	8.4	8.5 [m]
Saint Vincent and the Grenadines [i]	9.7	9.6	9.5	9.1	9.0	9.0	9.3	9.2	9.3	9.3 [m]
Suriname [x]	15.6	13.8	12.0	11.7	11.7	11.8	11.7	12.0	12.3	12.5 [c]
Trinidad and Tobago [i]	10.2	10.5	12.3	11.9	9.2	8.0	7.7	7.5	7.7	8.2 [c]

Source: Economic Commission for Latin America and the Caribbean (ECLAC), on the basis of official figures.
[a] Figures as of November.
[b] Local-currency loans to the non-financial private sector, at fixed or renegotiable rates, signature loans of up to 89 days.
[c] Figures as of October.
[d] Nominal local-currency rate for 60-91-day operations.
[e] Interest rate on total consumer credit.
[f] Non-adjustable 90-360 day operations.
[g] Weighted average of consumer, prime, ordinary and treasury lending rates for the working days of the month. Owing to the high turnover of treasury credit, its weighting was set at one fifth of the amount disbursed daily.
[h] Weighted average of the system lending rates in local currency.
[i] Weighted average of lending rates.
[j] Effective benchmark lending rate for the corporate commercial segment.
[k] Basic lending rate for up to one year.
[l] Average of highest and lowest lending rates.
[m] Figures as of September.
[n] Average of the rate of commercial banks credit cards and the average rate of mortgage credits.
[o] Weighted average of short-term lending rates in local currency.
[p] Interest rate on one-year trade credit.
[q] Commercial lending rate, local currency.
[r] Market lending rate, average for transactions conducted in the last 30 business days.
[s] Business credit, 30-367 days.
[t] Average rate for loan operations for the six major commercial banks.
[u] Weighted average of lending and overdraft rates.
[v] Figures as of August.
[w] Rate for personal and business loans, residential and other construction loans; weighted average.
[x] Average lending rate.

Table A.26
Latin America and the Caribbean: consumer prices
(12-month percentage variation)

	2006	2007	2008	2009	2010	2011	2012	2013	2014	2015 [a]
Latin America and the Caribbean [b]	4.8	6.3	8.3	4.6	6.5	6.9	5.7	7.6	9.5	...
Latin America and the Caribbean [c]	4.4	5.6	7.0	3.5	5.4	5.7	4.9	4.9	6.3	6.6
Latin America										
Argentina	9.8	8.5	7.2	7.7	10.9	9.5	10.8	10.9	23.9	14.3
Bolivia (Plurinational State of)	4.9	11.7	11.9	0.3	7.2	6.9	4.5	6.5	5.2	4.3
Brazil	3.1	4.5	5.9	4.3	5.9	6.5	5.8	5.9	6.4	9.9
Chile	2.6	7.8	7.1	-1.4	3.0	4.4	1.5	3.0	4.6	4.0
Colombia	4.5	5.7	7.7	2.0	3.2	3.7	2.4	1.9	3.7	5.9
Costa Rica	9.4	10.8	13.9	4.0	5.8	4.7	4.5	3.7	5.1	-0.9
Cuba [d]	5.7	10.6	-0.1	-0.1	1.5	1.3	2.0	0.0	2.1	1.7 [e]
Dominican Republic	5.0	8.9	4.5	5.7	6.3	7.8	3.9	3.9	1.6	1.2
Ecuador	2.9	3.3	8.8	4.3	3.3	5.4	4.2	2.7	3.7	3.5
El Salvador	4.9	4.9	5.5	-0.2	2.1	5.1	0.8	0.8	0.5	-0.2
Guatemala	5.8	8.7	9.4	-0.3	5.4	6.2	3.4	4.4	2.9	2.2
Haiti	10.3	9.9	10.1	2.0	6.2	8.3	7.6	3.4	6.4	11.7
Honduras	5.3	8.9	10.8	3.0	6.5	5.6	5.4	4.9	5.8	2.5
Mexico	4.1	3.8	6.5	3.6	4.4	3.8	3.6	4.0	4.1	2.5
Nicaragua	10.2	16.2	12.7	1.8	9.1	8.6	7.1	5.4	6.4	2.8
Panama	2.2	6.4	6.8	1.9	4.9	6.3	4.6	3.7	1.0	-0.4
Paraguay	12.5	6.0	7.5	1.4	7.7	4.9	4.0	3.7	4.2	3.2
Peru	1.1	3.9	6.7	0.2	2.1	4.7	2.6	2.9	3.2	3.7
Uruguay	6.4	8.5	9.2	5.9	6.9	8.6	7.5	8.5	8.3	9.2
Venezuela (Bolivarian Republic of) [f]	17.0	22.5	31.9	25.1	27.2	27.6	20.1	56.2	68.5	...
The Caribbean										
Antigua and Barbuda	0.0	5.2	0.7	2.4	2.9	4.0	1.8	1.1	1.3	0.6 [g]
Bahamas	2.3	2.8	4.5	1.3	1.4	3.2	0.7	0.8	0.2	2.0 [g]
Barbados	5.6	4.7	7.3	4.4	6.5	9.6	2.4	1.1	2.3	-0.3 [h]
Belize	2.9	4.1	4.4	-0.4	0.0	2.6	0.8	1.6	-0.2	-0.7 [g]
Dominica	1.8	6.0	2.0	3.2	0.3	1.9	1.3	-0.4	0.5	-1.7 [g]
Grenada	1.7	7.4	5.2	-2.3	4.2	3.5	1.8	-1.7	-0.6	-0.9 [g]
Guyana	4.2	14.1	6.4	3.6	4.5	3.3	3.4	0.9	1.2	-0.2 [g]
Jamaica	5.7	16.8	16.9	10.2	11.7	6.0	8.0	9.7	6.2	3.5 [i]
Saint Kitts and Nevis	8.0	2.9	6.5	1.2	5.2	2.9	0.1	0.3	-0.6	-2.7 [g]
Saint Lucia	-0.5	6.8	3.4	-3.1	4.2	4.8	5.0	-0.7	3.7	0.1 [g]
Saint Vincent and the Grenadines	4.8	8.3	8.7	-1.6	0.9	4.7	1.0	0.0	0.1	-1.8 [g]
Suriname	4.7	8.3	9.4	1.3	10.3	15.3	4.4	0.6	3.9	4.1
Trinidad and Tobago	9.1	7.6	14.5	1.3	13.4	5.3	7.2	5.6	8.5	4.8 [e]

Source: Economic Commission for Latin America and the Caribbean (ECLAC), on the basis of official figures.
[a] Twelve-month variation to October 2015.
[b] Weighted average.
[c] Weighted average, does not include the Bolivarian Republic of Venezuela.
[d] Refers to national-currency markets.
[e] Twelve-month variation to September 2015.
[f] Up to 2008, national consumer price index.
[g] Twelve-month variation to June 2015.
[h] Twelve-month variation to July 2015.
[i] Twelve-month variation to August 2015.

Table A.27
Latin America and the Caribbean: fiscal balances
(Percentages of GDP)

	Primary balance				Overall balance			
	2012	2013	2014	2015[a]	2012	2013	2014	2015[a]
Latin America and the Caribbean[b]	-0.1	-0.7	-0.4	-0.7	-2.1	-2.9	-2.6	-3.3
Latin America[c]	-0.2	-0.6	-1.0	-1.0	-1.9	-2.3	-2.8	-3.0
Argentina	-0.1	-1.4	-2.5	-0.8	-1.9	-2.6	-4.4	-2.6
Bolivia (Plurinational State of)[d]	2.7	2.0	-1.7	...	1.8	1.4	-2.5	...
Brazil	1.9	1.5	-0.3	-0.7	-1.8	-2.6	-5.3	-8.3
Chile	1.2	0.0	-1.0	-2.6	0.6	-0.6	-1.6	-3.3
Colombia	0.1	-0.1	-0.4	-0.4	-2.3	-2.3	-2.4	-3.0
Costa Rica	-2.3	-2.9	-3.1	-3.6	-4.4	-5.4	-5.6	-6.7
Cuba	...	...	...	...	6.7	1.9	0.6	-0.5
Dominican Republic	-2.8	-0.4	-0.1	0.5	-5.2	-2.7	-2.6	-2.5
Ecuador	-1.0	-4.5	-5.0	-1.2	-2.0	-5.8	-6.4	-3.0
El Salvador	0.5	0.6	0.8	1.4	-1.7	-1.8	-1.6	-0.7
Guatemala	-0.9	-0.6	-0.4	-0.8	-2.4	-2.1	-1.9	-2.1
Haiti	2.0	-1.0	-0.5	-2.6	1.7	-1.4	-0.9	-2.8
Honduras	-4.3	-5.8	-2.1	-0.9	-6.0	-7.9	-4.4	-3.9
Mexico[e]	-0.7	-0.5	-1.1	-1.3	-2.6	-2.4	-3.2	-3.5
Nicaragua	1.5	1.0	0.6	0.3	0.5	0.1	-0.3	-0.7
Panama	-0.7	-1.9	-2.7	-2.1	-2.6	-3.8	-4.4	-4.2
Paraguay	-1.4	-1.4	-0.7	-0.8	-1.7	-1.7	-1.1	-1.5
Peru	2.4	1.5	0.5	-1.7	1.3	0.5	-0.5	-2.6
Uruguay	0.4	0.9	-0.1	-0.5	-1.9	-1.5	-2.3	-2.8
Venezuela (Bolivarian Republic of)	-2.2	1.0	0.9	...	-4.9	-1.9	-1.6	...
The Caribbean[f]	0.1	-0.8	0.6	0.3	-3.2	-4.0	-2.7	-3.0
Antigua and Barbuda	1.1	-2.4	-0.6	-0.3	-1.3	-4.5	-3.3	-3.0
Bahamas[g]	-4.2	-3.2	-0.3	1.4	-6.6	-5.7	-3.3	-1.6
Barbados[h i]	-1.4	-4.1	0.7	-0.7	-8.0	-11.2	-6.9	-8.6
Belize[h]	1.5	0.9	-1.5	0.1	-0.4	-1.7	-4.2	-2.5
Dominica	-7.6	-7.4	-0.3	0.3	-9.2	-9.5	-2.1	-1.6
Grenada	-2.1	-3.4	-0.4	2.6	-5.5	-6.5	-3.9	-1.4
Guyana	-3.6	-3.4	-4.5	-2.3	-4.7	-4.4	-5.5	-3.3
Jamaica[h]	5.5	7.8	7.6	7.9	-4.2	-0.6	-0.5	-0.3
Saint Kitts and Nevis	17.2	17.1	13.0	...	11.2	13.2	9.9	...
Saint Lucia	-3.0	-2.9	0.8	-2.8	-6.5	-6.7	-3.0	-5.9
Saint Vincent and the Grenadines	0.3	-3.7	-1.6	...	-2.1	-6.2	-3.9	...
Suriname[j]	-1.8	-4.5	-4.5	-6.2	-2.7	-5.9	-5.4	-7.8
Trinidad and Tobago[k]	-0.4	-1.4	-0.9	-2.4	-2.1	-3.0	-2.5	-4.2

Source: Economic Commission for Latin America and the Caribbean (ECLAC), on the basis of official figures.
[a] Preliminary figures established on the basis of information from official budgets and estimates.
[b] Simple averages for the 33 countries reported. Coverage corresponds to central government.
[c] Simple averages. Does not include Cuba.
[d] General government.
[e] Federal public sector.
[f] Simple averages.
[g] Fiscal years, from 1 July to 30 June.
[h] Fiscal years, from 1 April to 31 March.
[i] Non-financial public sector.
[j] Includes statistical discrepancy.
[k] Fiscal years, from 1 October to 30 September.

Table A.28

Latin America and the Caribbean: central government revenues composition

(Percentages of GDP)

	Total revenue				Tax revenue			
	2012	2013	2014	2015[a]	2012	2013	2014	2015[a]
Latin America and the Caribbean[b]	22.8	22.8	22.7	22.6	17.8	17.6	17.9	18.1
Latin America[c]	18.9	19.2	19.3	18.7	14.8	14.9	15.2	15.3
Argentina	18.2	19.3	21.2	22.6	16.7	17.1	17.9	19.2
Bolivia (Plurinational State of)[d]	35.0	36.7	37.7	...	20.9	21.7	22.3	...
Brazil	22.3	22.2	22.1	21.6	19.7	19.7	19.9	19.1
Chile	22.3	21.1	20.7	20.5	19.0	18.2	18.1	18.5
Colombia	16.1	16.9	16.7	16.3	14.3	14.2	14.3	14.5
Costa Rica	14.4	14.4	13.9	14.1	13.5	13.6	13.2	13.3
Cuba	54.5	43.1	31.9	34.9	30.6	22.3	19.8	19.8
Dominican Republic	13.6	14.6	15.1	15.2	13.1	13.9	14.1	14.3
Ecuador	22.2	21.5	20.2	19.9	13.9	14.4	14.3	15.4
El Salvador	15.8	16.3	15.8	15.7	14.4	15.4	15.0	15.0
Guatemala	11.6	11.6	11.5	11.0	10.8	11.0	10.8	10.4
Haiti	13.4	13.3	13.2	15.1	12.9	12.2	12.1	14.1
Honduras	16.7	17.0	18.7	18.7	14.7	15.1	16.7	16.9
Mexico[e]	22.5	23.7	23.3	22.1	8.4	9.7	10.6	10.6
Nicaragua	17.8	17.4	17.5	17.5	15.1	15.2	15.4	15.3
Panama	16.2	15.4	14.2	14.1	11.1	10.8	9.8	10.5
Paraguay	19.0	17.1	17.9	18.4	14.3	13.1	14.4	13.9
Peru	19.2	19.2	18.8	16.3	16.5	16.4	16.3	14.3
Uruguay	19.9	20.7	19.9	19.6	17.9	18.2	17.7	17.6
Venezuela (Bolivarian Republic of)	23.5	25.8	28.1	...	13.2	13.0	15.2	...
The Caribbean[f]	26.0	26.5	26.9	27.5	21.3	21.1	21.8	22.0
Antigua and Barbuda	19.9	18.5	18.9	19.6	18.6	17.1	17.7	17.1
Bahamas[g]	16.4	17.2	20.7	23.0	14.8	14.8	18.6	20.9
Barbados[h][i]	27.8	27.3	28.8	29.2	26.0	25.2	26.7	26.6
Belize[h]	26.7	29.0	28.3	28.1	22.5	23.1	23.7	23.5
Dominica	27.7	28.0	29.3	34.4	23.1	22.2	22.1	23.6
Grenada	20.7	20.6	24.9	29.5	18.7	18.4	19.4	18.3
Guyana	24.7	23.6	23.6	26.4	20.3	20.6	21.4	22.2
Jamaica[h]	26.3	28.5	26.6	28.4	24.4	25.2	24.0	25.5
Saint Kitts and Nevis	42.6	46.3	41.1	...	20.2	19.8	20.6	...
Saint Lucia	23.7	24.5	25.3	26.8	20.9	22.6	22.6	23.4
Saint Vincent and the Grenadines	27.0	26.9	28.0	...	23.0	21.6	23.7	...
Suriname	24.3	22.6	21.1	20.3	18.3	17.9	16.1	16.4
Trinidad and Tobago[j]	29.8	31.0	33.4	33.2	26.4	26.2	27.1	24.7

Source: Economic Commission for Latin America and the Caribbean (ECLAC), on the basis of official figures.
[a] Preliminary figures established on the basis of information from official budgets and estimates.
[b] Simple averages for the 33 countries reported.
[c] Simple averages. Does not include Cuba.
[d] General government.
[e] Federal public sector.
[f] Simple averages.
[g] Fiscal years, from 1 July to 30 June.
[h] Fiscal years, from 1 April to 31 March.
[i] Non-financial public sector.
[j] Fiscal years, from 1 October to 30 September.

Table A.29
Latin America and the Caribbean: central government expenditure composition
(Percentages of GDP)

	Total expenditure				Interest payments on public debt				Capital expenditure			
	2012	2013	2014	2015[a]	2012	2013	2014	2015[a]	2012	2013	2014	2015[a]
Latin America and the Caribbean[b]	25.0	25.6	25.3	25.6	2.3	2.3	2.4	2.6	4.7	5.2	4.8	4.7
Latin America[c]	20.9	21.5	22.0	21.7	1.7	1.7	1.8	2.1	4.5	4.7	4.7	4.3
Argentina	20.1	21.9	25.6	25.2	1.7	1.2	1.9	1.8	2.1	2.8	4.3	3.0
Bolivia (Plurinational State of)[d]	33.2	35.4	40.2	...	0.9	0.6	0.8	1.0	10.8	13.5	16.6	...
Brazil	24.1	24.8	27.4	30.0	3.7	4.1	5.0	7.7	1.5	1.5	1.7	1.4
Chile	21.7	21.7	22.3	23.7	0.6	0.6	0.6	0.7	4.0	3.7	3.8	4.5
Colombia	18.4	19.2	19.1	19.2	2.4	2.2	2.1	2.6	2.8	3.1	3.0	3.0
Costa Rica	18.8	19.8	19.6	20.8	2.1	2.6	2.6	3.1	1.5	1.6	1.7	1.4
Cuba	47.8	41.1	31.4	35.3	...	...	...	...	8.8	7.4	3.1	4.0
Dominican Republic	18.8	17.3	17.7	17.7	2.4	2.3	2.5	2.9	5.6	3.3	2.7	2.6
Ecuador	24.2	27.3	26.6	22.9	0.9	1.2	1.4	1.7	10.5	12.2	11.7	9.0
El Salvador	17.5	18.1	17.3	16.5	2.2	2.3	2.4	2.2	3.3	3.0	2.8	2.8
Guatemala	14.0	13.8	13.4	13.1	1.5	1.6	1.4	1.4	3.3	3.0	2.9	2.6
Haiti	14.3	14.5	13.5	18.0	0.3	0.4	0.4	0.2	3.7	3.7	1.9	6.3
Honduras	22.7	24.9	23.1	22.5	1.7	2.1	2.3	3.0	4.6	5.2	5.2	4.2
Mexico[e]	25.1	26.0	26.5	25.7	1.9	1.9	2.0	2.2	4.8	5.5	5.2	...
Nicaragua	17.2	17.3	17.8	18.3	1.0	0.9	0.9	1.0	3.7	3.8	4.0	4.6
Panama	18.8	19.2	18.6	18.3	1.9	1.8	1.7	2.1	7.4	8.5	7.4	6.3
Paraguay	20.6	18.8	19.0	19.9	0.2	0.3	0.4	0.7	4.7	3.8	3.6	2.5
Peru	17.9	18.7	19.3	18.9	1.1	1.1	1.1	1.0	4.4	4.7	4.7	4.5
Uruguay	21.8	22.2	22.2	22.4	2.3	2.4	2.3	2.2	1.4	1.4	1.4	1.3
Venezuela (Bolivarian Republic of)	28.4	27.8	29.6	...	2.7	3.0	2.5	...	4.8	4.7	4.6	...
The Caribbean[f]	29.2	30.4	29.5	30.4	3.3	3.2	3.2	3.3	4.8	5.7	5.1	5.3
Antigua and Barbuda	21.3	22.9	22.2	22.6	2.5	2.0	2.7	2.7	0.6	1.3	1.7	2.2
Bahamas[g]	23.1	22.9	24.0	24.6	2.4	2.5	3.0	3.0	3.1	3.0	3.2	2.7
Barbados[h][i]	35.8	38.4	35.7	37.7	6.6	7.1	7.6	7.9	1.1	1.4	1.9	2.7
Belize[h]	27.1	30.8	32.4	30.6	1.9	2.6	2.7	2.6	4.6	6.8	7.6	5.6
Dominica	36.9	37.5	31.5	36.0	1.6	2.1	1.8	1.8	12.8	11.8	6.5	9.5
Grenada	26.2	27.1	28.8	31.0	3.4	3.1	3.5	4.0	5.0	6.8	9.1	12.2
Guyana	29.4	28.0	29.1	29.7	1.1	1.0	1.0	1.0	9.7	8.2	8.0	6.1
Jamaica[h]	30.4	29.0	27.1	28.7	9.7	8.4	8.1	8.2	2.9	3.1	1.5	1.9
Saint Kitts and Nevis	31.3	33.0	31.2	...	5.9	3.8	3.1	2.9	3.7	6.7	5.6	...
Saint Lucia	30.2	31.2	28.3	32.7	3.5	3.7	3.8	3.1	6.8	7.7	5.8	6.6
Saint Vincent and the Grenadines	29.0	33.0	31.9	...	2.4	2.5	2.3	2.3	2.9	7.8	5.8	...
Suriname	26.7	27.0	25.7	28.0	0.8	1.3	0.9	1.5	4.4	4.3	5.0	2.8
Trinidad and Tobago[j]	32.0	34.0	36.0	37.4	1.8	1.6	1.6	1.8	4.7	5.4	4.8	5.1

Source: Economic Commission for Latin America and the Caribbean (ECLAC), on the basis of official figures.
[a] Preliminary figures established on the basis of information from official budgets and estimates.
[b] Simple averages for the 33 countries reported.
[c] Simple averages. Does not include Cuba.
[d] General government.
[e] Federal public-sector.
[f] Simple averages.
[g] Fiscal years, from 1 July to 30 June.
[h] Fiscal years, from 1 April to 31 March.
[i] Non-financial public sector.
[j] Fiscal years, from 1 October to 30 September.

Table A.30
Latin America and the Caribbean: central government gross public debt
(Percentages of GDP)

	2006	2007	2008	2009	2010	2011	2012	2013	2014	2015 [a]
Latin America [b]	35.2	30.3	28.7	30.6	29.2	29.1	30.7	32.2	33.2	34.3
Argentina	51.8	44.4	39.2	39.6	36.1	33.3	35.1	38.8	42.8	43.7
Bolivia (Plurinational State of)	49.7	37.2	34.0	36.3	34.6	34.5	29.1	28.4	26.8	26.7
Brazil [c]	55.8	57.2	57.5	59.7	52.0	50.8	56.4	56.7	58.9	66.0
Chile	4.9	3.9	5.1	5.8	8.7	11.1	12.0	12.8	15.1	16.2
Colombia	40.3	36.6	36.2	38.0	38.6	36.5	34.6	37.1	40.0	39.5
Costa Rica	33.3	27.6	24.8	27.2	29.1	30.6	35.2	36.3	39.3	42.5
Dominican Republic	18.9	17.0	23.2	27.2	27.7	28.7	32.3	38.5	37.6	37.8
Ecuador	26.5	25.2	20.6	14.9	17.8	17.3	20.2	23.0	27.7	30.7
El Salvador	37.7	34.9	34.4	42.6	42.6	41.7	45.7	44.0	44.2	44.7
Guatemala	21.6	21.4	19.9	22.8	24.0	23.7	24.3	24.6	24.4	26.0
Haiti [d]	36.2	33.6	42.3	34.3	22.8	23.9	28.0	30.5	36.1	37.4
Honduras	28.7	17.4	20.1	23.9	30.4	32.5	35.4	43.8	42.3	45.0
Mexico [e]	20.2	20.6	24.0	27.2	27.2	27.5	28.2	29.8	31.8	34.7
Nicaragua	54.8	32.3	28.6	32.3	33.3	31.9	31.5	31.6	30.2	29.6
Panama	56.5	49.0	41.4	41.7	39.7	37.9	37.0	36.8	38.9	37.9
Paraguay	18.4	14.7	13.4	13.9	12.1	9.8	12.6	13.6	16.6	16.9
Peru	29.8	25.8	23.1	22.8	20.7	18.4	18.2	17.4	18.0	16.9
Uruguay	60.6	57.2	44.5	53.3	39.9	38.4	40.2	36.9	39.2	38.6
Venezuela (Bolivarian Republic of)	24.1	19.2	14.0	18.2	18.4	25.2	27.5	31.1	21.6	...

Source: Economic Commission for Latin America and the Caribbean (ECLAC), on the basis of official figures.
[a] Preliminary figures.
[b] Simple averages.
[c] General government.
[d] Data to September 2013. Does not include public sector liabilities owed to commercial banks.
[e] Federal government.

Table A.31
Latin America and the Caribbean: non-financial public sector gross public debt
(Percentages of GDP)

	2006	2007	2008	2009	2010	2011	2012	2013	2014	2015 [a]
Latin America and the Caribbean [b]	53.8	47.5	46.5	50.7	50.8	50.1	51.4	53.0	53.3	54.5
Latin America [b]	37.4	32.3	30.8	32.8	31.8	31.4	32.9	34.5	35.9	37.0
Argentina	51.8	44.4	39.2	39.6	36.1	33.3	35.1	38.8	42.8	43.7
Bolivia (Plurinational State of) [c]	55.1	40.7	37.2	39.5	38.1	33.7	31.3	30.4	29.5	29.2
Brazil [d]	55.8	57.2	57.5	60.9	53.6	50.8	56.4	56.7	58.9	66.0
Chile	9.9	8.7	11.6	12.1	14.7	17.8	18.9	20.5	24.2	25.3
Colombia	47.5	43.8	42.7	45.1	46.2	43.1	40.6	43.1	46.0	45.4
Costa Rica	38.3	31.8	29.7	34.0	35.7	38.1	42.6	44.5	47.9	50.7
Dominican Republic [e]	18.9	17.0	23.2	27.2	27.7	28.7	32.3	38.5	37.6	37.8
Ecuador	28.5	27.0	22.1	16.3	19.6	18.3	21.1	24.1	29.9	32.5
El Salvador	39.9	37.0	36.9	45.2	45.1	44.1	47.9	46.3	46.5	47.0
Guatemala	21.9	21.6	20.1	23.3	24.4	23.9	24.5	24.8	24.5	26.1
Haiti [e] [f]	36.2	33.6	42.3	34.3	22.8	23.9	28.0	30.5	36.1	37.4
Honduras [e]	28.7	17.4	20.1	23.9	30.4	32.5	35.4	43.8	42.3	45.0
Mexico [g]	22.2	22.4	26.5	34.3	31.7	34.4	33.9	36.8	40.3	45.5
Nicaragua	55.1	32.9	29.4	34.2	34.8	32.6	32.2	32.3	30.7	30.1
Panama	57.2	49.6	41.9	45.4	43.0	38.5	37.6	37.3	39.2	37.0
Paraguay [h]	21.2	16.8	15.5	16.8	14.9	11.5	14.2	15.1	18.6	18.8
Peru	33.9	29.9	26.9	23.7	23.5	22.1	20.4	19.6	20.1	20.0
Uruguay	65.4	62.5	48.9	49.4	43.5	43.4	45.7	41.5	44.6	43.9
Venezuela (Bolivarian Republic of) [e]	24.1	19.2	14.0	18.2	18.4	25.2	27.5	31.1	21.6	...
The Caribbean [b]	77.7	69.8	69.4	76.9	78.6	77.4	78.3	80.1	78.8	80.1
Antigua and Barbuda	90.5	81.1	81.5	95.7	87.1	86.7	89.4	95.1	95.4	103.3
Bahamas	36.2	36.9	37.4	44.1	45.7	50.2	54.5	59.1	65.8	62.0
Barbados	61.1	62.4	67.2	76.0	87.7	93.0	96.2	105.2	108.7	110.9
Belize	92.5	83.6	79.4	82.2	72.3	70.7	72.8	78.5	77.6	76.2
Dominica	89.4	81.2	72.0	66.4	73.1	70.7	72.7	75.5	74.1	76.0
Grenada	87.5	82.9	79.1	90.0	91.8	86.8	88.6	103.3	99.1	99.0
Guyana	97.3	61.2	62.9	67.0	68.0	66.7	63.6	58.1	50.1	53.8
Jamaica	117.8	110.9	112.3	126.3	131.7	131.4	133.9	135.5	132.7	130.7
Saint Kitts and Nevis	149.5	134.6	127.6	142.0	151.4	141.1	129.3	102.1	78.0	74.5
Saint Lucia	65.3	64.7	61.9	64.0	65.5	66.3	71.0	76.4	78.4	82.3
Saint Vincent and the Grenadines	62.3	55.5	58.4	64.7	66.7	65.5	67.0	64.9	72.2	76.0
Suriname	29.2	23.0	27.8	27.7	27.5	26.8	27.1	34.5	33.1	35.6
Trinidad and Tobago	32.1	28.8	34.5	54.4	53.8	50.1	52.4	52.9	58.6	61.4

Source: Economic Commission for Latin America and the Caribbean (ECLAC), on the basis of official figures.
[a] Preliminary figures.
[b] Simple averages.
[c] Refers to the external debt of the non-financial public-sector and central-government domestic debt.
[d] General government.
[e] Central government.
[f] Data to September 2013. Does not include public sector liabilities owed to commercial banks.
[g] Federal public-sector.
[h] Domestic debt includes liabilities owed to the central bank only.

Publicaciones recientes de la CEPAL
ECLAC recent publications

www.cepal.org/publicaciones

Informes periódicos / *Annual reports*
También disponibles para años anteriores / *Issues for previous years also available*

- Estudio Económico de América Latina y el Caribe 2015, 204 p.
  Economic Survey of Latin America and the Caribbean 2015, 196 p.
- La Inversión Extranjera Directa en América Latina y el Caribe 2015, 150 p.
  Foreign Direct Investment in Latin America and the Caribbean 2015, 140 p.
- Anuario Estadístico de América Latina y el Caribe 2014 / *Statistical Yearbook for Latin America and the Caribbean 2014, 238 p.*
- Balance Preliminar de las Economías de América Latina y el Caribe 2014, 92 p.
  Preliminary Overview of the Economies of Latin America and the Caribbean 2014, 92 p.
- Panorama Social de América Latina 2014, 296 p.
  Social Panorama of Latin America 2014, 284 p.
- Panorama de la Inserción Internacional de América Latina y el Caribe 2015, 102 p.
  Latin America and the Caribbean in the World Economy 2015, 98 p.

Libros y documentos institucionales / *Institutional books and documents*

- Desarrollo social inclusivo: una nueva generación de políticas para superar la pobreza y reducir la desigualdad en América Latina y el Caribe., 2015, 180 p.
  Inclusive social development: The next generation of policies for overcoming poverty and reducing inequality in Latin America and the Caribbean, 2015, 172 p.
- Guía operacional para la implementación y el seguimiento del Consenso de Montevideo sobre Población y Desarrollo, 2015, 146 p.
  Operational guide for implementation and follow-up of the Montevideo Consensus on Population and Development, 2015, 139 p.
- América Latina y el Caribe: una mirada al futuro desde los Objetivos de Desarrollo del Milenio. Informe regional de monitoreo de los Objetivos de Desarrollo del Milenio (ODM) en América Latina y el Caribe, 2015, 88 p.
  Latin America and the Caribbean: looking ahead after the Millennium Development Goals. Regional monitoring report on the Millennium Development Goals in Latin America and the Caribbean, 2015, 88 p.
- La nueva revolución digital: de la Internet del consumo a la Internet de la producción, 2015, 98 p.
  The new digital revolution: From the consumer Internet to the industrial Internet, 2015, 98 p.
- Panorama fiscal de América Latina y el Caribe 2015: dilemas y espacios de políticas, 2015, 128 p.
  Fiscal Panorama of Latin America and the Caribbean 2015: Policy space and dilemmas. Executive Summary, 2015, 14 p.
- Globalización, integración y comercio inclusivo en América Latina. Textos seleccionados de la CEPAL (2010-2014), 2015, 326 p.
- El desafío de la sostenibilidad ambiental en América Latina y el Caribe. Textos seleccionados de la CEPAL (2012-2014), 2015, 148 p.
- Pactos para la igualdad: hacia un futuro sostenible, 2014, 340 p.
  Covenants for Equality: Towards a sustainable future, 2014, 330 p.
- Integración regional: hacia una estrategia de cadenas de valor inclusivas, 2014, 226 p.
  Regional Integration: Towards an inclusive value chain strategy, 2014, 218 p.
  Integração regional: por uma estratégia de cadeias de valor inclusivas, 2014, 226 p.
- Reflexiones sobre el desarrollo en América Latina y el Caribe. Conferencias magistrales 2013-2014, 2014, 100 p.
- Cambio estructural para la igualdad: una visión integrada del desarrollo, 2012, 330 p.
  Structural Change for Equality: An integrated approach to development, 2012, 308 p.
- La hora de la igualdad: brechas por cerrar, caminos por abrir, 2010, 290 p.
  Time for Equality: Closing gaps, opening trails, 2010, 270 p.
  A Hora da Igualdade: Brechas por fechar, caminhos por abrir, 2010, 268 p.

Libros de la CEPAL / *ECLAC books*

137 Juventud: realidades y retos para un desarrollo con igualdad, Daniela Trucco, Heidi Ullmann (eds.), 2015, 282 p.

136 Instrumentos de protección social: caminos latinoamericanos hacia la universalización, Simone Cecchini, Fernando Filgueira, Rodrigo Martínez, Cecilia Rossel (eds.), 2015, 510 p.

135 *Rising concentration in Asia-Latin American value chains: Can small firms turn the tide? Osvaldo Rosales, Osvaldo, Keiji Inoue, Nanno Mulder (eds.), 2015, 282 p.*

134 Desigualdad, concentración del ingreso y tributación sobre las altas rentas en América Latina, Juan Pablo Jiménez (ed.), 2015, 172 p.

133 Desigualdad e informalidad: un análisis de cinco experiencias latinoamericanas, Verónica Amarante, Rodrigo Arim (eds.), 2015, 526 p.

132 Neoestructuralismo y corrientes heterodoxas en América Latina y el Caribe a inicios del siglo XXI, Alicia Bárcena, Antonio Prado (eds.), 2014, 452 p.

131 El nuevo paradigma productivo y tecnólogico: la necesidad de políticas para la autonomía económica de las mujeres, Lucía Scuro, Néstor Bercovich (eds.), 2014, 188 p.

Copublicaciones / *Co-publications*

- Gobernanza global y desarrollo: nuevos desafíos y prioridades de la cooperación internacional, José Antonio Ocampo (ed.), CEPAL/Siglo Veintiuno, Argentina, 2015, 286 p.
- *Decentralization and Reform in Latin America: Improving Intergovernmental Relations, Giorgio Brosio and Juan Pablo Jiménez (eds.), ECLAC / Edward Elgar Publishing, United Kingdom, 2012, 450 p.*
- Sentido de pertenencia en sociedades fragmentadas: América Latina desde una perspectiva global, Martín Hopenhayn y Ana Sojo (comps.), CEPAL / Siglo Veintiuno, Argentina, 2011, 350 p.

Coediciones / *Co-editions*

- Perspectivas económicas de América Latina 2015: educación, competencias e innovación para el desarrollo, CEPAL/OCDE, 2014, 200 p.
  Latin American Economic Outlook 2015: Education, skills and innovation for development, ECLAC,/CAF/OECD, 2014, 188 p.
- *Regional Perspectives on Sustainable Development: Advancing Integration of its Three Dimensions through Regional Action, ECLAC-ECE-ESCAP-ESCWA, 2014, 114 p.*
- Perspectivas de la agricultura y del desarrollo rural en las Américas: una mirada hacia América Latina y el Caribe 2014, CEPAL / FAO / IICA, 2013, 220 p.

Cuadernos de la CEPAL

101 Redistribuir el cuidado: el desafío de las políticas, Coral Calderón Magaña (coord.), 2013, 460 p.

101 *Redistributing care: The policy challenge, Coral Calderón Magaña (coord.), 2013, 420 p.*

100 Construyendo autonomía: compromiso e indicadores de género, Karina Batthyáni Dighiero, 2012, 338 p.

Documentos de proyecto / *Project documents*

- Complejos productivos y territorio en la Argentina: aportes para el estudio de la geografía económica del país, 2015, 216 p.
- Las juventudes centroamericanas en contextos de inseguridad y violencia: realidades y retos para su inclusión social, Teresita Escotto Quesada, 2015, 168 p.
- La economía del cambio climático en el Perú, 2014, 152 p.
- La economía del cambio climático en la Argentina: primera aproximación, 2014, 240 p.

Cuadernos estadísticos de la CEPAL

42 Resultados del Programa de Comparación Internacional (PCI) de 2011 para América Latina y el Caribe. Solo disponible en CD, 2015.

41 Los cuadros de oferta y utilización, las matrices de insumo-producto y las matrices de empleo. Solo disponible en CD, 2013.

Series de la CEPAL / *ECLAC Series*

Asuntos de Género / Comercio Internacional / Desarrollo Productivo / Desarrollo Territorial / Estudios Estadísticos / Estudios y Perspectivas (Bogotá, Brasilia, Buenos Aires, México, Montevideo) / *Studies and Perspectives* (The Caribbean, Washington) / Financiamiento del Desarrollo/ Gestión Pública / Informes y Estudios Especiales / Macroeconomía del Desarrollo / Manuales / Medio Ambiente y Desarrollo / Población y Desarrollo/ Política Fiscal / Políticas Sociales / Recursos Naturales e Infraestructura / Seminarios y Conferencias.

Revista CEPAL / *CEPAL Review*

La Revista se inició en 1976, con el propósito de contribuir al examen de los problemas del desarrollo socioeconómico de la región. La *Revista CEPAL* se publica en español e inglés tres veces por año.

CEPAL Review first appeared in 1976, its aim being to make a contribution to the study of the economic and social development problems of the region. CEPAL Review is published in Spanish and English versions three times a year.

Observatorio demográfico / *Demographic Observatory*

Edición bilingüe (español e inglés) que proporciona información estadística actualizada, referente a estimaciones y proyecciones de población de los países de América Latina y el Caribe. Desde 2013 el Observatorio aparece una vez al año.

Bilingual publication (Spanish and English) proving up-to-date estimates and projections of the populations of the Latin American and Caribbean countries. Since 2013, the Observatory appears once a year.

Notas de población

Revista especializada que publica artículos e informes acerca de las investigaciones más recientes sobre la dinámica demográfica en la región. También incluye información sobre actividades científicas y profesionales en el campo de población.
La revista se publica desde 1973 y aparece dos veces al año, en junio y diciembre.

Specialized journal which publishes articles and reports on recent studies of demographic dynamics in the region. Also includes information on scientific and professional activities in the field of population.
Published since 1973, the journal appears twice a year in June and December.

Las publicaciones de la CEPAL están disponibles en:
ECLAC publications are available at:

www.cepal.org/publicaciones

También se pueden adquirir a través de:
They can also be ordered through:

www.un.org/publications

United Nations Publications
PO Box 960
Herndon, VA 20172
USA

Tel. (1-888)254-4286
Fax (1-800)338-4550
Contacto / *Contact*: publications@un.org
Pedidos / *Orders*: order@un.org

www.ingramcontent.com/pod-product-compliance
Lightning Source LLC
Chambersburg PA
CBHW080244270326
41926CB00020B/4365